Homemade Candle Making Recipes

Natural Homemade Candle Making Recipes Book With Step by Step Exposition on How to Make candle for absolute Beginners and Beyond

BY
EMMA WILLIAMS

Copyright © 2019 by Emma Williams

All rights reserved. No part of this book may be used or reproduced by any means, graphic, electronic, or mechanical, including photocopying, recording, taping, or by any information storage retrieval system, without the written permission of the publisher except in the case of brief quotations embodied in critical articles and reviews.

Table of Contents

Candles: History and Perspective 1

1: DIY Color Block Crayon Candle 7

2: DIY Layered Scent Candles 9

3: DIY Mason Jar Candle 11

4: DIY Pumpkin Chai Soy Candle 13

5: Pretty Chai Candle in Canning Jars 15

6: DIY Scented Candle 17

7: DIY Candle Melts with Essential Oil 19

8: DIY Gingerbread Wood Wick Candle 21

9: DIY Cinnamon Bun Candle 23

10: DIY Beach Sand Covered Votive Candles 26

11: DIY Crockpot Candles Rosemary and Lavender 28

12: DIY Hot Chocolate Candle 30

13: DIY Teacup Candle 32

14: DIY Funfetti Candle 34

15: DIY French Vanilla Candle 36

16: DIY Citronella Candle 38

17: DIY Pineapple Candle 40

18. DIY Glitter Candle 42

19: DIY Massage Candle 44

20: DIY Champagne Flute Candle 46

21: DIY Apple Spice Candle 48

22: DIY Satsuma Candle 50

23: DIY Watermelon Candle 52

24: DIY Cookie Cutter Candle 54

25: DIY Lemon Lavender Aromatherapy Candle 56

26: DIY Mosquito Repellent Candle 58

27: DIY Citronella Floating Candle 60

28: DIY Beer Candle 62

29: Rolled Beeswax Candles 64

30: DIY Bottle Cap Candle 66

31: DIY Water Candle 68

32: DIY Eco Friendly Soy Candle Favors 70

33: DIY Lavender Candle 72

34: DIY Survival Candle 74

35: DIY Gel Candle 76

36: DIY Grapefruit Fir Candle 78

37: DIY Valentines Day Candle 80

38: DIY Pumpkin Spice Candle 83

39: DIY Beeswax Candle in Mason Jar 85

40: Eucalyptus Essential Oil Candle 88

41: DIY Sea Shell Candle 90

42: DIY No Wax Candle 92

43: Dried Flower Candles 94

44: DIY Floral Candle 96

45: DIY Beeswax Tea Light Candle 98

46: DIY Spiced Beeswax Autumn Candle 100

47: DIY Marbled Easter Egg Candles 103

48: DIY Ombre Candle 105

49: DIY Mug Candle 107

50: DIY Soy Wax Candle 109

51: DIY Forest Pine Candle 111

52: DIY Tin Punched Votive Candle 113

53: DIY Sea Glass Candle 115

54: Coffee Scented Candles 117

55: DIY Poured Herbal Candle 119

56: Lemon Beeswax Candle 121

57: DIY Tissue Paper Candle 123

58: DIY Starbucks Candle 125

59: DIY Hidden Gem Candle 127

60: Wood Wick Teacup Candles 129

61: DIY Floating Halloween Candle 131

62: DIY Gilded Birthday Candle 134

63: DIY Metallic Colored Candle 136

64: DIY Color Flame Candle 138

65: DIY Pillar Candle 140

66: DIY Holiday Candle Favors 143

67: DIY Glitter Pumpkin Candle 145

68: DIY Fruit Scraps Candle 147

69: DIY Manly Candle 149

70: Wine Bottle Drip Candle Holder 151

71: DIY Citronella Beeswax Candle 153

72: DIY Wine Bottle Candle 155

73: DIY Sand Candle 157

74: DIY Dip Dyed Candle 159

75: DIY Olive Oil Candle 161

76: DIY Ice Candle 163

Conclusion 165

Candles
History and Perspective

What role do candles play in your life? Since they were first invented, their role in human societies continues to diversify. In the beginning, it was all about light. Of course, the meaning of light is as diverse as it is essential to our existence. A candle may play a different role in your life today, tomorrow or the next day. Just how profoundly have candles affected human development functionally, culturally and spiritually?

Retail sales for candles in the U.S. for 2001 were approximately 2.3 billion dollars. Candles are used in seven out of 10 U.S. households. The majority of candle consumers burn candles between one and three times per week and burn one to two candles at a time. There are over 300 known commercial manufacturers of candles in the U.S. alone.

What elements constitute or define a candle? The essential elements of early candles were a wick, fuel and container or mount. Aromatherapy and colorants have become common editions to most modern candles. Candles have been used for thousands of years but until the 20th century, their essential and primary purpose was to provide artificial light. Today, the applications for candles are so broad and diverse; they have become an integral part of our everyday lives.

Egyptians

It is fair to assume that controlling and capturing fire to produce artificial light on demand has been an obsession since early man first discovered fire. The first known records of this process begin with the ancient Egyptians. Clay candle holders dating from the 4th century B.C. have been found in Egypt. Egyptians eventually used rush lights or torches. They made these torches by soaking the pithy core of reeds in molten tallow. Tallow is the fatty tissue or suet of animals. The tallow of cattle and sheep was routinely used because it became hard. There was no wick involved in these early candles.

Romans

The people of the Roman Empire were the first to use candle wicks. They melted tallow to a very liquid state and poured it over flax, hemp or cotton fiber which created a wick. These candles provided artificial light for utilitarian purposes and were also used in religious ceremonies. There were two primary problems with the use of tallow. It produced both a terrible odor and smoke. Tallow did not burn cleanly.

Asian

Early Asian cultures extracted wax from insects (coccos pella) and seeds and then molded it in tube containers of plant paper. The Japanese extracted wax from tree nuts to create candles. In China, beeswax was used during the Tang Dynasty (618-907 A.D.).

India

Early Indian cultures extracted wax from boiling cinnamon and created tapered candles. These candles were used in Indian Temples.

Middle Ages

By this time, beeswax had been discovered. Although harder to acquire, this was a great improvement because the beeswax produced a subtle sweet smell and burned cleanly. These candles were highly valued by the clergy and upper classes that were among those who could access/afford them.

North America

In the first century A.D., Native Americans burned oily fish that were called candlefish. Missionaries that eventually settled the southwestern United States boiled bark from the Cerio tree to extract wax for candle making. Colonial women in New England discovered they could boil the grayish green berries of bayberry bushes and extract wax. This was a difficult and tedious process but the bayberry wax burned sweetly and cleanly. In the late eighteenth century, the whaling industry developed. Spermaceti wax, a whale product that had a mild odor and was harder than both tallow and beeswax made candles available to more people. Many historians claim that the first "standard candles" were made using spermaceti wax.

The Industrial Age

1834

Mass production came to candle making. Joseph Morgan invented a machine that used a cylinder featuring a piston that ejected candles as they solidified in their molds.

1850

Paraffin wax was invented. It is processed by distilling the residues left behind by the refining of crude petroleum. This bluish-white wax burned cleanly and with no unpleasant or much odor of any kind. It was also cheap to produce.

20th Century

Eventually, stearic acid was added since it was discovered this ingredient in the original tallow candles was what maintained a higher melting point and produced a harder candle. The growth of the meatpacking and oil industries made candles a common necessity. In 1879, the electric light bulb was invented. However, history did not end for the development of the candle. This was just a temporary setback that reinvented the mission and the market for candles.

Modern Chandlers (Candle Makers)

Internationally, paraffin remains the most popular candle fuel although the use of stearic wax is mostly practiced in Europe. However, technology continues to develop candles that offer new and more benefits. In 1992, after much testing Michael Richards made the first all-vegetable candle wax which has developed into our modern soy candle. The versatility of this wax allows for use in both low-melt container candles and high temperature melt for free standing pillar candles.

Gel candles

The most recent state-of-the-art technology revolves around gel candles. The gel is a combination of polymer resin and mineral oil. The patent for making gel wax is held by Penreco Corporaton (US Patent 5,879,694) and is called versagel. Gel provides exceptional safety in terms of its flash point. It is best used in creating what is known as a hurricane candle by putting it in a decorative translucent container and adding a wick. Due to the clarity of the gel, these candles produce 40% more luminescence than regular paraffin wax. Modern chandlers turned artists, now produce beautiful collectibles in the form of embedded glass candle designs. The gel can be reinstated, and the candle passed down through generations to be used again and again.

So...What role do candles play in your life?

Well, they can still light a room...but they can also light a heart. They can express love that lasts a lifetime and an infinite collection of special moments and appreciation. Candles are a cultural, technical, artistic, therapeutic and spiritual expression of the finest moments in human evolution and experience. That is why they are still present in our lives...in spite of the electric light bulb. This article invites you to use them to celebrate life in all its creative glory.

Should You Learn to Make Your Own Candles?

These days, there are as many candle companies as there are candle scents to choose from. Some companies have wonderful products, while others are less than desirable in both product and service. With decent candles available at local department stores and online, why would you want to make your own candles? Candle making is a fun and affordable hobby. Candle lovers spend hundreds of dollars annually on ready-made candles, so why not learn how to make them yourself and perhaps not only save some money, but learn a new skill and develop a pleasurable past-time?

We are all familiar with the basic paraffin wax candle. There are, however, many different types of candle waxes that can be used to make candles. Beeswax, soy, and other vegetable blend waxes are available on the market that makes candle creation easier and healthier for everyone. Natural waxes such as soy are safer not only in the fact that the wax does burn when touched, but also because when burned it does not emit toxic fumes into the air. There are also many decorative and useful containers that you can use to create candles in. Mason jars are a very popular candle container. You can also learn how to make decorative candles that look and smell like food and desserts. Your choices are really limited only to your imagination and ability level.

Some basic information about candle making is to have a safe area in which to make candles. Especially important when you're first learning, a safe and ventilated area will ensure you learn the process correctly from the beginning and will not cause harm to yourself or your home. If you have a wax spill, just make sure to clean it up fast so you aren't risking getting hurt from falls or having a big mess afterward.

Most people begin learning how to make candles with the simple votive candle. These useful little candles are easy to make and you can experiment with colors and scents. You can use this learning time to see what you like, what works and what doesn't and also learn different wax temperatures and cooling processes. By starting off simple, you can enjoy learning and not risk getting frustrated and quitting before you become good at making candles.

Learning to make your own candles at home will save you money and give you a relaxing hobby once you have the process down pat. Don't get frustrated if your first efforts at candle making are less than what you expected. Like anything, practice and patience will pay off with a beautiful, useful product that you can proudly display in your home or perhaps even turn into a profitable home business.

So, you want to create your own candles. But how do you start and what is the simplest way to begin? The answer is... the 75 candle making recipes below.

We know how daunting the prospect of creating candles on your own for the first time might be, but with the candle making recipes we have provided it will be sheer fun.

No stress, little mess. And did I mention having "fun"? Of course I did!

1

DIY Color Block Crayon Candle

Crayons play a huge role in childhood and recently they have even become popular among people of all ages (thank you, adult coloring books!). It's not surprising that most people have bags of unused crayons laying around their house, but this super cute DIY can give them a different purpose. Whether you use old crayons you already have or buy a new box, you'll fall in love with these color block crayon candles.

What you'll need:

- Dixie cups
- Wax
- Crayons
- Wicks
- Votives
- Popsicle sticks
- Plate stand

Directions:

1. Pour a small amount of wax into a Dixie cup and microwave for 1 minute. Stir with a popsicle stick and pour thin layer onto bottom of a votive. Place a wick in the center and let harden.

2. Peel paper off three different crayon colors you want to use. Fill three Dixie cups with wax and break up each crayon in separate cups. Microwave the wax right before you use it for two minutes and stir then microwave for another two minutes.

3. Prop the votives on the plate stand so it's on an angle. Pour in the colored wax you want to be at the bottom. Wait 20-30 minutes for the first layer of wax to harden.

4. Turn votives around to pour the second layer of wax color on a different angle. Let it dry for 20-30 minutes then take votive off plate stand to put on flat surface.

5. Fill up the votive with the third layer of wax color and wait one hour for it to dry before lighting it.

2

DIY Layered Scent Candles

They are so much fun to make. (And super easy too!) The really great thing about these DIY holiday candles is that each layer is not only a different color, but also a different holiday scent. So as the candles burn, the delicious scent of peppermint, or balsam or frankincense wafts through the air.

What you'll need:

- Soy wax flakes
- Crayons in assorted colors

- Small heat-proof jars
- Wicks
- Essential oils

Directions:

1. Choose the number of layers you want to create for each candle. Divide the wax evenly. I used about 3/4 to 1 cup wax flakes per layer (so about 1/3 to 1/4 cup per layer, per jar.) Remove the papers from the crayons and break into small pieces. Melt soy wax flakes and crayons in a pan. Slowly stir in 5-10 drop of the desired essential oil.
2. Adhere the wicks to the bottoms of the jars using a little melted wax. Wrap the wick around a skewer or toothpick to keep it centered.
3. Pour the first color layer into the jars. Let cool completely. You can speed up the process by placing them outside or in a cool place.
4. Repeat the process with more wax, crayons, and essential oils. To keep the new layer from melting the previous layer, it is helpful to let the wax cool slightly before pouring into the jar.
5. After the last layer is poured into the jar, let the jars sit undisturbed for several hours or overnight. Trim the wicks, top with the lids, and package up to give away.

3

DIY Mason Jar Candle

Making mason jar candles is as easy as melting wax and pouring it into a jar with a wick. There are a few tips and tricks along the way that I will share with you, but never fear, this project is suitable for even a beginner crafter. Pick your scent to personalize the candle then dress them up with fabric, tulle, raphia and of course, some beautiful labels!

What you'll need:

- 1200 g soy wax
- 12 waxed wicks with tabs

- Candle scent
- Heat proof 100g canning jars
- A double boiler
- Hot glue gun
- Thermometer
- Crayon pieces or wax dye (optional)

Directions:

1. Prepare your jars by adding a bit of hot glue onto the bottom of the wick tab and press it firmly into the center of your container. If your fingers won't fit into the jar, use a pen or straw around the wick to stick the tabs down.
2. Assemble your double boiler and add wax to the top pot. Heat over medium heat until the wax is completely melted.
3. If you are adding colour, add at this stage by dropping in bits of crayon or wax dye until you are happy with the look keeping in mind it will be lighter and more opaque when dry.
4. When the wax reaches 140°F it's time to add the fragrance. Pour in 5ml per 1lb of wax and stir well to mix.
5. Cool wax to 110°F and carefully pour into jars. Prop up the wicks with a chopstick or clothes pin to keep them centered.
6. Wrap a towel around the outside of the jars and set aside to cool. Be careful not to disturb the candles too much while they set. Cooling slowly and completely will create the best looking candles.
7. Trim the wicks to ¼" above the wax.
8. Allow your candle to cure for 48 hours undisturbed before burning.

4

DIY Pumpkin Chai Soy Candle

I could seriously burn pumpkin candles all year. This DIY Pumpkin Chai Candle has both calming and uplifting properties that are perfect for anti-anxiety and stress. This candle is also made with natural soy wax and it smells amazing. I made a printable label that you can download later in this post and use for a gift.

What you'll need:

- Wide Mouth Mason Jar
- 4 cups Soy Wax
- Candle Wick

- Pumpkin Spice Essential Oil
- Vanilla Essential Oil
- Ginger Essential Oil
- Clove Essential Oil
- Hot Glue Gun
- Free Printable Label
- Wooden Jar Lid

Directions:

1. Start by applying hot glue to the metal tab on the candle wick. Place the tab in the bottom center of a glass jar and let the hot glue set. I used a new clamping method with two popsicle sticks and a clothespin. This is the best way I have found to hold the wick in place. Set aside.
2. Place 4 cups of natural soy wax flakes into a heat resistant bowl. Using the double boiler method, melt the wax until completely dissolved into a liquid. I added 1 oz of pumpkin spice essential oil, 1 oz vanilla essential oil and 10 drops of clove and ginger essential oils to the melted wax. You can add desired amount of oils.
3. Pour the scented liquid candle wax into the prepared jar. Set aside and let harden.
4. The candle wax will change to a white color once it is completely set and hardened. Trim the wick by cutting it with a pair of scissors.

5

Pretty Chai Candle in Canning Jars

These DIY chai candles in canning jars are a pretty, natural way to bring some autumn cheer inside. They are delicately scented with baking spices – ginger, cardamom, cinnamon and nutmeg – that will warm your home. Chai promotes therapeutic healing according to Ayurvedic philosophy and medicine by calming, vitalizing and mentally clarifying.

What you'll need:

- 14-15 ounces soy wax flakes per candle
- ½ teaspoon each: ground ginger, cardamom, allspice, cinnamon and nutmeg

- Two ½ pint canning jar
- Two candle wicks
- Chopsticks or skewers
- An old pan or clean can for melting wax

Directions:

1. Place wax flakes in a double boiler or large glass measuring cup in the microwave.
2. Dip the end of the candle wicks into the melted wax and adhere to the center of the bottom of the jars. Wrap the wicks around chopsticks or skewers set over the top of the jar to keep the wicks centered.
3. Once wax has almost melted, remove from heat and stir to finish melting. Add the spices and stir well. (Some will sink to the bottom of the jar).
4. Pour the wax into the prepared jars, leaving a little space at the top. Let cool completely.
5. Trim the wick to desired length and use or give as a gift.

6

DIY Scented Candle

Smell is one of our most powerful senses, with the ability to evoke nostalgia, whet your appetite or instill calm. Everything you need to make them is available online, and affordable too, but a lot of this stuff you will have at home. Once you nail this recipe, they will be your go-to gift, as you can personalize the scents.

What you'll need:

- 2kg soy wax or paraffin
- scented or essential oils or mica or candle powders in various colours (optional – the amount you'll need depends on the desired colour, so start with 1/2 teaspoon and go from there)

- Double boiler (or use a heatproof bowl and a saucepan)
- thermometer
- Candle moulds (for example small glass jars, tins and pots)
- Spray oil
- Wicks
- Hairdryer

Directions:

1. Begin by grating or chopping your wax or paraffin. The smaller you chop it, the quicker it will melt. If you are using a double boiler, get it set up.
2. If you don't have one, boil some water in a large saucepan, then set heatproof bowl on top of the saucepan.
3. Add the wax to the top of the boiler or the bowl and leave to melt, stirring every so often. Use a thermometer to ensure the temperature of the wax does not exceed 90°C.
4. Once the wax has melted, add your desired oil or combination of oils (for a 250ml-sized candle, about 30ml of oil is ample) and powder for colour, if you wish. I would do this over the heat, very quickly, so that the colouring agent combines easily.
5. Remove from the heat once everything has been added and mixed so that the colour and oil are distributed evenly. Set aside and quickly prep your mould.
6. If you're using a temporary mould, spray it with a little oil for easy removal.
7. Next, insert the wick by tying the wick to a pencil and sitting it horizontally across the top of the mould so that the wick hangs vertically.
8. Pour in the wax to about 2cm from the top. The candle sometimes shrinks in the centre, so you can add a little more wax if needed. Use a hair dryer to dispel any air bubbles or divots, and smooth the top.
9. Cut off the wick and leave the candle for at least 24 hours before removing from the mould or lighting it if using a permanent mould.

7

DIY Candle Melts with Essential Oil

Essential oil-based candles not only emits flame but also adds a natural ambiance to a room, making you feel warm, cozy, and calm. The joy of lighting a candle and the benefits of aromatherapy goes hand in hand.

Making candles is easy because it involves only melting the wax and pouring it into a jar. You can add your touch to it by adding aroma and color to it.

What you'll need:

- Containers/jars
- Essential oils
- Wick-centering tool
- Soy wax
- Candle wicks -make sure the wick is taller than your container
- Large glass measuring cup
- Something to stir wax with like an orangewood stick

Directions:

1. Take the jar to prepare the candle.
2. With the help of wax, anchor the wick in the center of the jar and secure it using a clip or pen or a chopstick. Let the wick be longer than the jar at this point of time.
3. Melt the wax in a microwave-safe container or a pot over medium heat. Make sure that the wax melts fairly well. Stir at regular intervals.
4. Once the wax evenly melts, measure the wax in a measuring flask.
5. Add 10 to 20 drops of essential oil to the wax and stir to blend it well.
6. Pour the wax into the candle jar and make sure that it spreads evenly without any bubbles or dip.
7. Adjust the wick to the center and secure it using a clip.
8. Let the wax stand still until it solidifies.
9. Cut the wick to an optimal length.
10. Keep your candle closed using a cloth or box for two days before burning it.

8

DIY Gingerbread Wood Wick Candle

Easy melt and pour soy-based gingerbread candle with wood wicks. Great for gift giving!

What you'll need:

- 2 cups soy candle wax flakes

- 40-50 drops gingerbread scented oil
- 2 wood wicks
- 2 4 oz glass containers

Instructions:

1. Begin by placing newspaper down for any spills. Hot glue or use stickers to place your wicks in the center of the jars you are using and set aside.
2. In a microwave safe bowl melt the 2 cups of candle flakes in 30-45 second intervals. My wax melted in about 5 minutes total but microwave time may vary. You can also melt the wax using a double boiler on the stove. Use pot holders and caution when removing the hot wax.
3. Allow the wax to cool slightly and add in the gingerbread scented oil.
4. Slowly pour your scented wax into the glass containers.
5. Let the candles sit for 24 hours without disturbing.
6. Trim the wicks to 1/4 inch

9

DIY Cinnamon Bun Candle

I especially love something that can be whipped together in no time at all, and for less than $10 to boot! These candles make our home feels so warm and cozy, but they can cost a pretty penny, especially the decorative ones. That is where I had the idea for this cute cinnamon candle DIY.

Warning: they can be a little addictive to make and you may want to make one for every room in the house. They also make perfect handmade gifts for the holidays. Check out how crazy easy they are to make below.

What you'll need:

- 11 oz. Pillar of Bliss Wax
- 1 oz. Cinnamon Bun Fragrance Oil
- Red Liquid Candle Dye
- Brown Liquid Candle Dye
- Cd-14 Wick
- Votive Wick Pin
- Pouring Pot
- Bakery Style Cinnamon Bun Mold
- Blow Dryer
- Pen/Pencil
- Glass Plate

Directions:

1. Clean & Sanitize your work area and all of your packaging materials. It is suggested that you wear gloves, protective clothing, and a hair net while preparing this recipe.
2. Weigh out 10 oz. of Pillar of Bliss Wax on scales.
3. Place the wax into a pouring pot.
4. Once all the wax is in a liquid state, place 3 drops of brown liquid candle dye to the melted wax. Using a toothpick, place a very small amount of red liquid candle dye to the melted wax. Stir.
5. Add 3/4 oz. of Cinnamon Bun fragrance oil to melted wax and stir.
6. Pour prepared melted wax into cinnamon bun mold. Allow to set up completely.

7. Once candle is set up, remove from mold.

8. Weigh out 1 oz. of Pillar of Bliss Wax on scales.

9. Place the wax into a pouring pot. Using the double boiler method from before, melt wax on low on the stove until the wax is completed melted.

10. Set your wick pin down on a flat sturdy surface. Carefully centering the Cinnamon Bun candle over top of the wick pin, slowly push the wick pin through the candle by gently forcing the candle down on top of the wick pin

11. Get your wick, and place it through the centered hole.

12. Add 1 teaspoon of Cinnamon Bun fragrance to your melted wax. Stir.

13. Place your cinnamon bun candle on a glass plate and slowly pour the melted wax over the top to simulate icing. Allow this to harden.

14. Using a pen/pencil, curl the top of the wick.

10

DIY Beach Sand Covered Votive Candles

A trip to the beach is a lot like a trip to the craft store! There are so many natural elements available for crafting and being creative, and sand has a beautiful and unexpected texture to add to your decor. Making a sand covered candle votive is extremely easy, and looks simple and striking.

What you'll need:

- A selection of glass votives or glass covered candles with labels pulled off.

- Elmer's Glue
- Sand! Maybe it's from the beach your currently visiting, or maybe it's from the craft store. Be aware – very course sand wont work as well as fine sand for this craft.

Directions:

1. Wash any sticky glue left over from labels on your candle glassware, let dry.
2. Thickly apply Elmer's glue to small sections of the votive at a time.
3. Dip into your sand, and then move to a new section.
4. Check for any areas that need more sand, and once the votive is fully covered, gently tap it on your counter to allow the excess sand to fall off.
5. Dry for 48 hours and enjoy! Feel free to add ribbon or glue shells on the votive if that's your style. I personally love it simple and spare!

11

DIY Crockpot Candles Rosemary and Lavender

It took me FOREVER to finally decide I could make these Easy DIY Crockpot Candles. I have no idea why because it's super easy and y'all adding essential oils just makes them so much better than store bought candles. These Lavender and Rosemary crockpot candles turn out so pretty.

What you'll need:

- Glass jars
- Soy wax flakes
- Weighted candle wicks, large
- Rosemary oil
- Lavender oil OR dried lavender
- Crockpot
- Scissors
- Chopstick or stirring stick

Directions:

1. Place the wick in the jar. If you need help getting it to stay centered, add a tad of glue to the weight and press into place.
2. Fill to the top with the soy flakes. Keep the wick centered as you fill.
3. Add 7-10 drops of rosemary oil to the jar. Place the jar in the crock pot set on high.
4. As the wax melts down, you will add more. Just sprinkle it in evenly around the wick.
5. Allow the jar to sit for about 60-90 minutes in the crock pot until the wax has liquefied. Add additional flakes as needed.
6. When the wax nears the top, sprinkle in the dried lavender buds. Or, you can add some of the lavender oil at this time.
7. Give the candle a last good stir, and remove from the pot. Allow to cool and harden.
8. Snip off any extra wick before burning. Never burn any candles unattended or do crafts with hot wax around children.

12

DIY Hot Chocolate Candle

With the colder weather having arrived by now, I've decided it's time to celebrate with a candle! This candle is really gorgeous and smells fantastic. It'd make a really great gift for a friend or family member too. It's really simple (and cheap!) to make and they're easy to make in bulk too.

They look just like hot chocolate and it's a really novel thing to have around, plus once all the wax has melted you can reuse the mug!

What you'll need:

- Mug

- Candle wick
- Soy wax
- Brown crayon
- Sprinkles
- A pencil or two
- Microwavable measuring cup
- Chocolate candle fragrance

Direction:

1. Prepping your mug, so make sure your mug is clean and place your wick inside your mug, the silver metal bit should be on the bottom of your mug.

2. So you're going to get a whole bunch of your wax and put it, with your brown crayon, in a microwave-proof measuring cup. Put your measuring cup into your microwave and microwave wax for 20 seconds at a time stirring in between, until your wax is the consistency of milk.

3. Add like four teaspoons of the chocolate candle fragrance, and if it still doesn't feel like enough, or you can't really smell it, add more.

4. So now you're going to take some more wax and melt it in your microwave, taking it out every 20 seconds and stirring it. This wax is going to be your whipped cream so you don't want to make it to thin, wait till it's the consistency of whipped cream, so still kinda lumpy and then pour it onto your brown wax. Add sprinkles whilst the wax is not yet set.

5. Allow the wax to set and then trim your wick to about a centimeter above your wax. Light that candle!

13

DIY Teacup Candle

Vintage teacups that have lost their saucers can make cute gifts when fitted with candles

What you'll need:

- Glue gun

- Candle thermometer (or you can also use a candy thermometer)
- Pre-waxed wire wick with clip
- Creme wax and or pieces of old candle
- Bag clippers or bamboo sticks
- Scent for candles (you can do rose, vanilla, lavender, etc.)
- Vintage tea cups (or any other container you like)
- Double boiler (the important thing is that the water is not to touch the glass container)

Directions:

1. Set the double boiler with water, cut wax and place it inside container. Hook on the thermometer. Burner on high.
2. Glue the wire core wick clip using the glue gun at the bottom of the containers you are using.
3. Hang wick by off a bamboo stick so that the wick is nice and straight. You can also use a bag sealer clip to grab the wick, it just needs to be long enough.
4. Once the wax is melted and gets to about 83°C, remove from heat and add color. Wait until it gets to 80°C and add scent.
5. Pour the wax into each container making sure the wick stays in place. Checked them regularly over the next half an hour or so to make sure the wick is still in place. And voila!

14

DIY Funfetti Candle

Are you looking for a fun snow day DIY or a simple craft to do with friends? Then look no further! These funfetti candles are fun to make AND fun to smell! If you want your room to smell like cupcakes, then this DIY is just what the doctor ordered!

What you'll need:

- 2 16oz mason jars
- Candle wicks
- Hot glue gun
- Pencils or something similar to hold the wicks in place

- Tape
- 2-3 tbsp water
- 1-2 tbsp corn syrup
- A small paintbrush or cloth
- 1/2 cup colorful sprinkles
- 1 lb soy wax flakes
- Cupcake scented wax cubes

Directions:

1. Hot glue the wick attachment to the bottom of the jar.
2. In a bowl, mix the corn syrup and water.
3. Coat the inside of the jar with the mixture and use a paintbrush to get all of the nooks and crannies.
4. Slowly add sprinkles to the jar and roll them around to get it evenly coated.
5. Lay a pencil across the top of the jar and tape the wick to it to keep it centered.
6. In a double boiler, melt the wax flakes and a few of the scented cubes.
7. Use a measuring cup with a spout to pour the wax into the jars.
8. Make sure to pour the wax into the center of the jar to avoid messing the sprinkles up.

Viola! There you have it, two yummy-smelling candles that look good enough to eat!

15

DIY French Vanilla Candle

These candles smell great and are easy to make

What you'll need:

- Small bowls or glasses
- Candle wax (you can find some at any craft store)

- Candle wick
- Coffee beans
- Vanilla beans, chopped

Directions:

1. Using a double broiler or a microwave safe bowl, melt the wax.
2. Glue the wick in place at the bottom of the cup or just hold it in place with your hand (at the top, of course).
3. Pour in a small layer of wax and add a layer of coffee beans and vanilla beans.
4. Then fill the rest of the cup with wax.
5. You can stir wax with a chopstick to distribute the bean pieces if needed. Then let the wax harden and trim the wick.

16

DIY Citronella Candle

You can never be over prepared when it comes to bugs and mosquitoes, keep these annoying pests away with natural citronella oils in a homemade candle. Making your own candles is really easy and you can usually find most of what you need to make them laying around the house.

What you'll need:

- Ceramic or Metal Pots, Jars or Containers

- Wax
- Citronella oil
- Candle Wicks
- Clear Tape
- Pencils or Sticks (To Keep Wicks Upright While They Set)
- Double Boiler

Directions:

1. Place all of your wax into the double boiler and heat the wax over a medium heat until it has all melted. This usually takes between 15 to 30 minutes depending on the type of wax being used.
2. Add the citronella oil and any other oils if you wish to slow down the burn rate of your candles. Stir the oil in well.
3. Place one wick into each of the jar and tape the end to the centre of the bottom of the jar to keep the wick in place. Use a tablespoon and drop a few spoons of wax onto the taped area to really secure the wick and keep the tape from pulling loose.
4. Place a pencil or stick across the top of the jars and rest the wick on it in an upright position.
5. Now pour the hot wax into the jars, fill the jars to about 2cm (1") from the top.
6. Once all of the jars are filled, place them in a sheltered and warm place with a dish towel around them and allow them to cool. You want them to cool as slowly as possible to prevent the wax from cracking.
7. Once they are cool, allow them to stand and cure for 48 hours before using them. Trim the wicks to 1cm (1/2") before lighting them.

17

DIY Pineapple Candle

This adorable candle looks and smells like a cute, little pineapple. It's super easy & fun for the whole family.

What you'll need:

- Candle wicks
- Candle wax pitcher
- Soy wax flakes
- Wax colorant
- Pineapple fragrance oil
- Black paint
- Green paint
- Paintbrush
- Green Felt
- Hot glue gun
- 6 oz glass jars

Directions:

1. Attach the candle wicks to the center of the bottom of the glass jars by using a drop of hot glue
2. Melt 4 cups of soy wax flakes in the candle pitcher over low-medium heat, stirring frequently
3. Add 3 blocks of yellow wax colorant and 20-30 drops of pineapple fragrance oil to the mixture. Combine.
4. Pour the wax into the glass jar. Let candles sit until completely cooled.
5. Dip your thin paintbrush into the black paint and draw small "V"'s around the glass jar to imitate the spikes of a pineapple.
6. Cut a zig-zag down the middle of your green felt. Roll up the two pieces and glue them to the lid of the candle jar to imitate the crown of the pineapple.

18. DIY Glitter Candle

Creating your own gold glitter and polka dot candles is easy to do with a few paper crafting supplies. I'm going to show you how to transform plain flameless candles into trendy gold candles in less than 5 minutes!

What you'll need:

- Candle
- Double-sided tape
- Fine craft glitter
- Plate, tray or piece of paper

Directions:

1. Place a strip of double-sided tape around the bottom of your candle. We kept it simple and chic with a glitter border around the bottom of the candle, but you can create any design you like with the double-sided tape.

2. Place a plate or piece of paper underneath the candle to catch the glitter. Pour the fine craft glitter onto the double-sided tape. *Tip: Reuse the excess glitter on the plate to glitter additional candles.

3. Place your candle on a heat-resistant surface, light and enjoy!

19

DIY Massage Candle

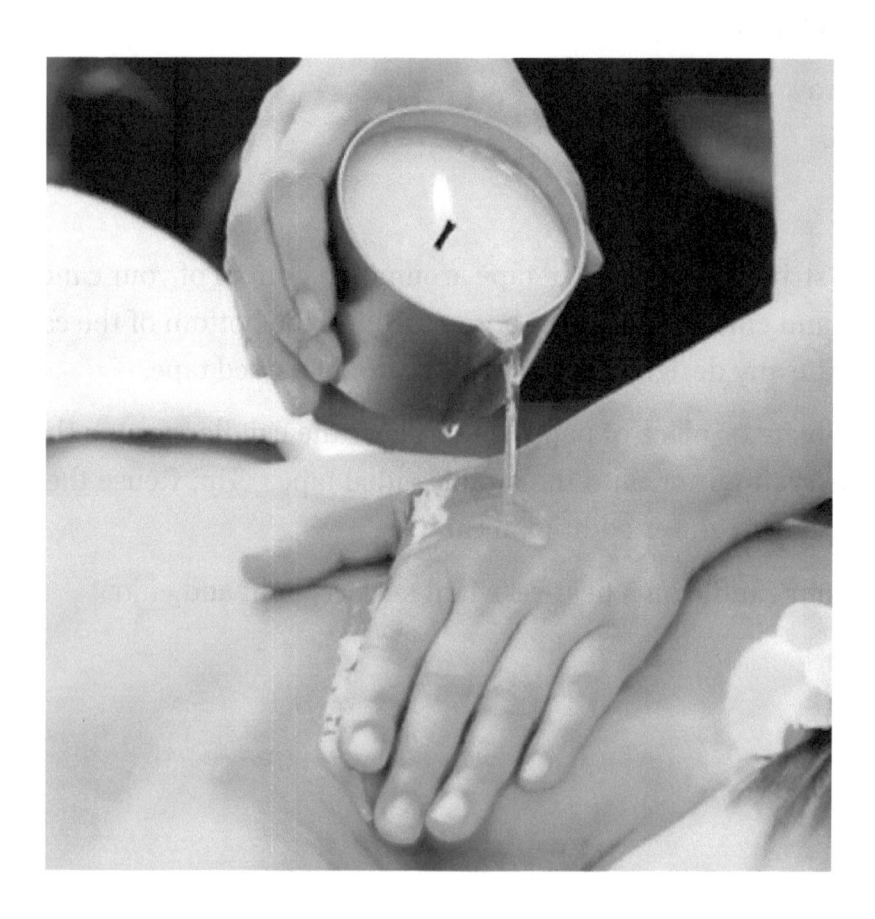

A concept so genius, yet so simple that I can't believe I didn't come up with it on my own: massage candles. In essence, they're candles made of wax so pure and nourishing that you can actually use it to moisturize your skin as the candles burn. A gorgeous candle and a luscious moisturizer all in one. I think we've just struck gold.

What you'll need:

- 1 part natural beeswax or soy wax
- 1 part natural cocoa butter or shea butter
- 1 part liquid carrier oil such as sweet almond or jojoba
- Essential oils of your choice (I used lavender and ylang ylang; use about 2-5 drops per ounce)
- Vessel of choice
- Candle wick
- Double boiler Cheese grater or knife
- Wooden stick for mixing

Directions:

1. Place your wick into your candle vessel and set aside.
2. Grate your wax and butter, or cut into small pieces. This increases the surface area, allowing your mixture to melt more quickly and evenly.
3. Turn on your double boiler. Over medium heat, gently mix the wax, butter, and carrier oil together with a wooden stick until fully melted. This could take anywhere from 2-10 minutes. Be careful not to mix too quickly, as this could cause air bubbles.
4. Remove from heat, add your essential oils, and mix again.
5. Pour the mixture into your vessel. Add support to hold up your candle wick if necessary – I used two wooden chopsticks.
6. As the mixture cools, you'll see it turn from a liquid to a solid right in front of your eyes! Mine took about 15 minutes altogether. Leave it alone during the cooling period. Once it has cooled, your candle is ready to be used!

20

DIY Champagne Flute Candle

Did you know making candles is a very easy process and you can really get creative on what you make your candles in? Take an old mug, candy dish, candle votive, champagne flute or anything else with a solid base and turn it into a fantastic DIY Candle.

What you'll need:

- Champagne Flutes (if you don't have any check your local thrift store)
- Soy Wax

- Candle Wicks
- Dixie Cups

Directions:

1. Grab your champagne flutes and rinse them out with warm water. Dry your glasses and set on a flat surface to air dry for a few moments. I'm sure yours are dusty like mine. (Don't judge!)

2. Now grab your Dixie cup and fill it with just a little bit of your soy wax and place in the microwave for 1 minute.

3. Remove your cups from the microwave and pour in the bottom of your champagne flutes. Quickly place your candle wicks into the wax and it will harden around the base of the wick within seconds.

4. Once the wax has hardened it's time to make up the rest of our candle.

5. Grab 3 dixie cups and fill them to the very top with your soy wax and place in the microwave for 2 minutes. Once your 2 minutes are up remove the Dixie cups from the microwave and immediately pour it into your candle base.

6. 3 Dixie Cups were enough for each champagne flute, so you'll need a total of 6 full cups to complete this project and that's it.

21

DIY Apple Spice Candle

An apple spice candle adds a festive fall fragrance in your home. This one is homemade so it's free of any harmful chemicals. Plus it's easy to make! I've been thinking about making homemade candles as Christmas gifts, and this apple spice candle would be well received, I'm sure!

What you'll need:

- 2 cups of soy wax flakes
- 1 candle wick w/weighted bottom

- 1 red crayon
- 1 teaspoon of apple pie seasoning or 5-7 drops of apple scented essential oil
- 1 teaspoon of cinnamon
- Wooden spoon
- Chopstick or pencil
- Glass teacup

Directions:

1. Begin by heating the soy wax flakes on low heat on the stove top. Use a nonstick pot for best results and quick and easy clean up.
2. Continue to stir the flakes as they melt. You want to keep the liquid moving.
3. You can now tint the soy flakes with a red crayon. DO NOT use food coloring as it will clump and not distribute in the mixture. Peel the crayon and break it into small pieces. Drop it into the mixture and stir. As the crayon melts the color will blend. 4. Add in the apple pie spice or oil as well as the cinnamon. Stir well. You will notice that the mixture will darken.
4. Wrap the top of the wick around a pencil or chopstick to hold it in place. Set the pencil over the top of the tea cup, allowing the wick to drop to the bottom.
5. Remove the mixture from the heat and slowly pour it into the cup. Adjust the wick if needed.
6. Store the candle in a cool place until it sets. Do not touch it while it is setting. Even if the top looks firm, the inside could be soft. Instead, let it sit for a full 3-4 hours before touching.
7. Once hardened, you can snip the wick to shorten it. Light the wick and enjoy!

22

DIY Satsuma Candle

This is a wonderfully simple yet very pretty DIY that I discovered on a blog I like - Honestly WTF Here is my take on the idea, its dead easy but so effective! Here is my take on the idea, its dead easy but so effective!

What you'll need:

- 1 satsuma
- 2-3 teaspoons Olive Oil

- Knife or scalpal
- Spoon
- Lighter

Directions:

1. Start by using the scalpal or knife and cutting just above the middle of the satsuma. Make sure you use the side with the green stem (green nobly bit) on, as the base as this is where the wick will be.

2. Your candle should now looks like this. I then used the scalpal to loosen the edges, and used a spoon to scoop out the centre (There's no waste if you enjoy eating satsumas)

3. At the bottom of the satsuma, there is enough pith which will act as your candle wick. Use a paper towel to lightly wipe away excess water and juice.

4. Now add a few drizzles of oilve oil, until the wick is almost, but not quite covered. You will now want to dip the wick into the oil for a few seconds which will make it easier to light.

    And there you have it. A stunning glowing satsuma, made from natural ingredients. Remember never to leave candles unattended! :)

23

DIY Watermelon Candle

It may surprise you how many designs you can create with candles. Making a watermelon candle is much like making any other kind of candle. The only difference is you make a few additional pours with some extra touches in the beginning. These candles are the perfect gift. They are unique, cute and handmade with love by you!

What you'll need:

- Black candle dye
- Green Candle dye

- Red candle dye
- Wax
- small paint brush
- 8 oz square mason jars

Directions:

1. In a large bowl, melt red crayon shavings with wax. In a smaller bowl, melt green crayon shavings with wax. In another small bowl, melt plain wax (will turn out white).
2. Prep cups by hot gluing the wick to the bottom of the paper cup.
3. Mix in citronella oil to all melted wax bowls.
4. Starting with the green wax, fill cup ¼ full. Place in fridge to cool wax quickly.
5. Next, pour a thin layer of plain white wax. Place in fridge to cool wax quickly.
6. Finally, fill cup the rest of the way with red wax and let cool.
7. When everything is dry, trim the wick, and peel off the cup.
8. If you want to add details, draw on seeds with a sharpie marker.

24

DIY Cookie Cutter Candle

Set the mood of the night with these DIY candle table decorations. We bet you've got most of the prep items lying around the house already!

What you'll need:

- Metal cookie cutters
- Masking tape
- Scissors

- Aluminium foil
- Petroleum jelly
- Double boiler
- Craft sticks (for stirring)
- Thermometer
- Metal-tabbed tea-light wicks
- Beeswax

Directions:

1. To turn a cutter into a mold, run masking tape along the edge, snip at the corners, and fold the tape outward so the cutter sits flat on the foil.
2. Coat molds with petroleum jelly; set aside. Place beeswax in double boiler over barely simmering water. Stir wax as it melts with craft sticks.
3. When wax reaches pouring temperature (150 degrees for paraffin, 160 degrees for beeswax, or as soon as a film forms at the edge of the pan, pour into molds. Carefully lower in the tea-light wicks. After candles harden (1/2 hour to 2 hours), lift them out by their wicks. If they resist, freeze until they pop out easily.
4. Wipe candles clean with paper towels.
5. Trim wicks, if necessary, to 1/4 inch before lighting.

25

DIY Lemon Lavender Aromatherapy Candle

How can one not love the scent, never mind the taste of lemon and lavender. Whether you are baking and enjoying the scents or burning a fragrant aromatherapy candle, it is pure joy!

We have found a wealth of knowledge on aromatherapy, essential oils and recipes using essential oils from the

What you'll need:

- Beeswax (6-8 oz)

- Essential Oil (I used 2 ml patchouli and 2 ml vetiver)
- 4 oz glass jar
- 1 wick
- A set of chop sticks
- Pyrex measuring cup
- Small soup pot
- 10 ml graduated cylinder (optional)

Directions:

1. Measure 6 oz. of beeswax (1 and 1/2 jar full). If you want the candle to fill right to the top use 8 oz. (2 jars full).
2. Wipe your Pyrex cup with jojoba.
3. Melt the beeswax in the Pyrex (see video for details).
4. Place the wick in the jar using the chop sticks shown in the video.
5. Measure your essential oil.
6. Once the beeswax is melted, add the essential oil to the beeswax and stir.
7. Pour slowly into the glass jar so to not disturb the wick.
8. Allow it to solidify for several hours before burning.

26

DIY Mosquito Repellent Candle

Tired of mosquito's hanging around your patios? ME TOO! You guys need to try these homemade mosquito repellent mason jar candles. They actually work better than the candles you can buy at the store!

What you'll need:

- 7 Drops Orange Essential Oil
- 12 Ounce Mason Jars
- 8 Ounces Water

- 1 Slice Fresh Orange
- 1 Slice Fresh Lime
- 1 Sprig of Fresh Rosemary
- 1 Tea Candle

Directions:

1. Place the water in your jar.
2. Place the slice of orange and slice of lime inside the jar, up against the sides.
3. Slide the rosemary sprig alongside the slice of orange so it stays up against the jar.
4. Add your essential oil to the water.
5. Remove the metal casing from around the tea light. If you have a floating candle, that will work as well. The metal casing should tear away pretty easily.
6. Pull the wick up off the candle and use it to place it in the water.
7. Light the candle and you're set!

Notes: A wide mouth mason jar will work better if you prefer your candle to float more in the middle. If you decide to use the jars similar to mine, you can add a bit more water so the ingredients don't impede the floating candle. I liked my candle being more secure so I used to ingredients to keep it from moving a lot. This ensured the candle didn't get too much liquid on it so it wouldn't go out. Any citrus essential oil or citronella oil will work.

27

DIY Citronella Floating Candle

Spruce up your summer social with this beautiful DIY citronella candle. It is not only EASY but it will change the look of any table AND it actually WORKS!

Did you know that many of those store-bought citronella candles don't actually contain citronella oil? Instead, the candles are often just citronella 'scented.' BIG difference.

What you'll need:

- Glass bowl or container

- Decorations of your choice. You can use anything! (Lemon peels, orange peels, cinnamon sticks, lavender, rosemary, flower petals, river rocks, etc.)
- 20 drops Citronella Essential Oil
- 10 drops Lemongrass Essential Oil
- 1 T Witch Hazel
- Water to top off glass bowl or container
- 1 unscented floating candle

Directions:

1. Gather decorations and arrange in a bowl. I recommend cutting them into two-inch pieces so they don't bunch at the top of the bowl or cause it to overturn.
2. Add Witch Hazel, Citronella, and Lemongrass Essential Oil to the bowl.
3. Fill in the remaining bowl space with water.
4. After placing your bowl outside, top it off with the floating candle and light it to create a cozy, aromatic ambiance you and your guests can enjoy throughout the evening.

28

DIY Beer Candle

I LOVE candles and almost always having one burning when I'm home. A few months ago I found Brewed2Burn candles, which are amazing. There's not beer in them, but they're all designed to smell like styles of beer like stouts, IPAs, etc.

I decided to try to replicate the brewery's cappuccino stout, Hold the Foam. It's one of my favorites. It smells just like a coffee shop.

What you'll need:

- Melting pot
- Beer can

- Coffee (brewed)
- Vanilla scent/flavor (either essential oils or vanilla extract
- Food coloring (optional)
- Soy wax
- Stirrer
- Can opener
- Pliers

Directions:

1. Remove the beer lid using a can opener and pliers, remove your can lid. Set it off to the side.
2. Melt the wax, add the coffee, vanilla. The amount of wax you use depends on the size of your beer can. I'm using a 16oz can, so I need 13oz of liquid soy wax, 3oz of coffee, and a splash of vanilla.
3. Once it's melted, pour in your coffee. Make sure you get some grounds in there too as it helps permeate the scent when the candle burns.
4. Pour the wax into the beer can. Anchor your wick to the bottom of the beer can with hot glue.
5. Then, pour your wax and coffee combo into the beer can while holding up the wick. Put two knives on each side of the wick to hold it in place.
6. Let the wax harden.
7. When you're done, you'll have a lovely smelling beer candle that will make your house smell like coffee.

29

Rolled Beeswax Candles

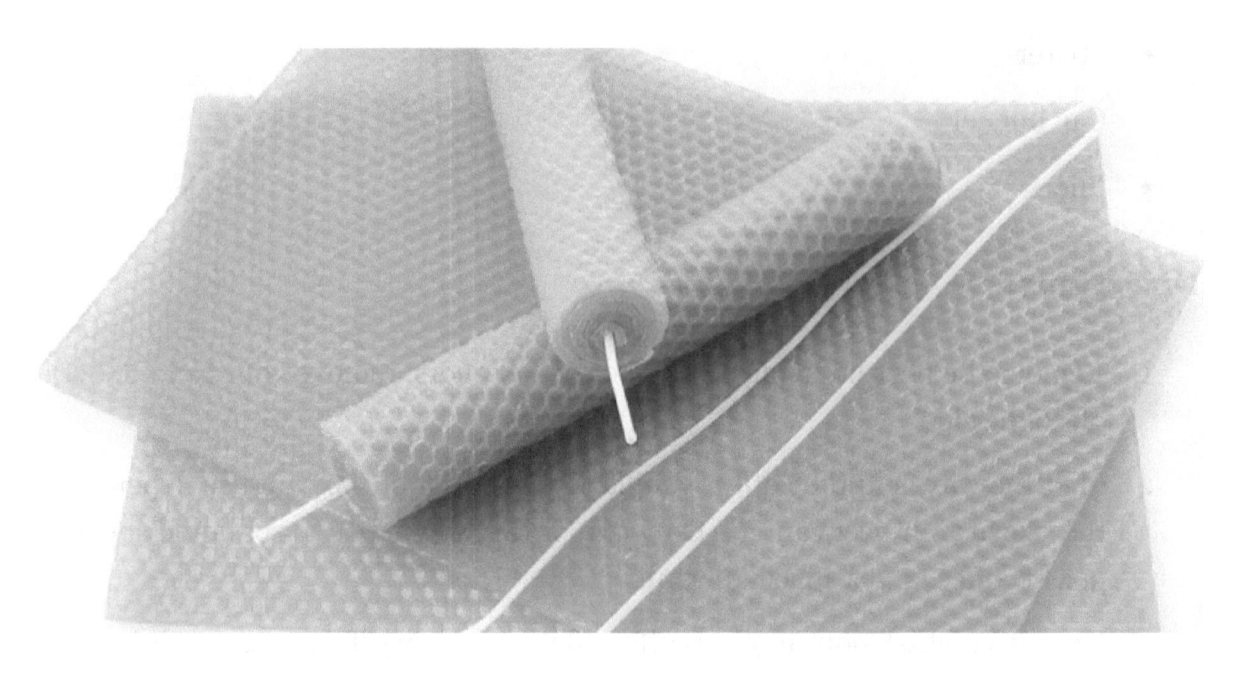

Rolled beeswax candles produce a warm, sweet scent, whether burned or kept intact. Their natural, honey-yellow color is sometimes dyed, opening decorative possibilities. Beeswax sheets for rolled candles mimic the natural honeycomb pattern by melting the wax and pressing it with molds. The result is a decorative wax that burns with little smoke.

What you'll need:

- Wax paper or baking parchment
- 2 or more honeycomb beeswax sheets, 8-inch by 16-inch, complementary or contrasting colors

- 1 waxed or primed candle wick, 2/0 gauge, 10 inches long
- Scissors
- Utility knife
- Stencils (optional)
- Blowdryer (optional)

Directions:

1. Spread a sheet of wax paper or baking parchment on a flat work surface.
2. Place a 8-inch by 16-inch sheet of honeycomb beeswax on the paper with an 8-inch-long end of the sheet toward you.
3. Lay a 10-inch piece of waxed, 2/0-gauge candle wick across the end of the beeswax sheet closest to you. Align the wick approximately 1/4 inch in from the end of the sheet and leave an equal amount of wick past the left and right sides of the sheet.
4. Press the wick into the wax with gentle pressure using your fingertips.
5. Roll and tuck the end of the wax sheet around the wick from left to right, forming a snug tube with the wick through its center.
6. Push the tube forward approximately 1/2 inch, keeping the left and right sides straight.
7. Roll the tube in small increments using gentle pressure, keeping the ends aligned, until you reach the end of the wax sheet.
8. Choose which end of the candle you prefer for the top. In most cases, one end looks tidier than the other. Trim off the excess wick up to the base of the candle with scissors, leaving the wick tail long at the top end.

30

DIY Bottle Cap Candle

Small bottle cap candles are great for an evening at the beach, a party in the garden, a BBQ on the porch, or when camping on vacation. Any occasion will do.

Bottle cap soy wax candles are so easy to make, and each candle should burn 1 to 1.5 hours.

What you'll need:

- Bottle Caps
- Soy Wax
- Candle Scent Block, Vanilla

- Yaley Concentrated Candle Dye Block: Lavender
- Natural Candle Wick

Directions:

1. Cut one inch pieces of wick. Use Elmer's glue or hot glue to attach the wick to the center of the bottle cap. For best results, use a wick with a clip, but if you don't have a clip (like me) this is a way to improvise. Let the glue dry completely before moving to step two.
2. Melt the wax. I have a warming plate that I use, but there are several DIY versions you can try if you don't have a melter. One of the most common techniques is to place a glass jar or recycled tin can in a pot of boiling water till the wax melts.
3. Once the wax has melted, add the colored wax. The concentration is very intense, so start with a tiny bit (shave or cut it off the larger cube), and add more color until you've achieved the desired effect.
4. Add the scented wax to the melted, colored wax. Again, start with a small amount then add more until the scent is pleasing to you.
5. Pour the melted wax into the bottle cap, and let it cool. Work on a craft sheet or wax paper to make clean up easier.

31

DIY Water Candle

Water Candles can be made in water glasses, wine glasses, vases, small fish tanks etc. They look fantastic, burn for a long time and will cost you less than dollar!

What you'll need:

- Glass cup
- Water
- Lamp oil or Cooking oil

- Candlewick
- Compass
- Scissor
- Tape
- Transparent Sheet
- Food Coloring
- Marbles
- Small Stones

Directions:

1. Take a transparent sheet and using a compass, draw a circle of around 1-2cm radius and make a hole in the center of it.
2. The second step is to cut the circle out you made in the first step.
3. Now, thread the transparent circle with a wick and the extra wick out.
4. Use a transparent tape to fic the wick to the circle.
5. Take a "teardrop" shaped glass or any shape you like, and put some marbles inside the glass.
6. In the next step, pour water into the glass cup.
7. Now, pour lamp oil into the glass cup.
8. Put the wick on top of the glass.
9. Finally, light up the wick using a lighter or matchstick.

   Your DIY water candle is all set to radiate your centerpiece! Enjoy your new level creativity with this water candle.

32

DIY Eco Friendly Soy Candle Favors

Do you think that your eco-friendly conscious won't let you impart nothing but a eco-friendly wedding favors to the wedding guests of yours? If so, then this DIY is just made for you to try and finish. It will teach you that how you can make the soy candle wedding favors using only the materials that are recycled with some added natural elements of course. These soy candle favors at the same time would be a very cheap method to show your love to your wedding participants

Only and only the eco-friendly items are needed for this process of making the eco friendly favors. And here are all of what you will have to gather before you start with the steps:

What you'll need:

- A wick
- Soy wax (flakes)
- Recycled jars
- Natural fragrance oil
- Chopsticks

Directions:

1. Take a non-stick pan or just a simple pan and melt the soy wax in it. As the soy was melts do add some of the natural oil fragrance and natural dye (if you wish to add some color to your soy candles).
2. Now leave the molten wax to cool down in the pan only.
3. Wash and dry the recycled jars that you have chosen as the containers for your soy wax candles.
4. Pour the wax into these jars with the chopstick in the middle attached with the wick. Leave about a quarter inch of wick on the upper part of the wax layer.
5. Take an eco-friendly ribbon or the paper and make tags out of it to make the favors more personalized; write down the names of the wedding guests to whom you will be presenting these favors.
6. Cover the jars with a cotton cloth piece (cut in a rounded or a square shape).
7. Tie a ribbon to the neck of the jar with the cloth along.
8. If you like then you can put an additional label denoting the name of the scent that the jar is carrying to the top of the cloth.

33

DIY Lavender Candle

Scented candles are always a lovely way to add an inviting feel to any room – especially lavender. But you don't need to spend a fortune on a store-bought designer variety, or spend hours messing about with hot wax – here's a clever hack to create your own personalized flower candle and celebrate your garden's most beautiful blooms in under half an hour.

What you'll need:

- A glass candle jar
- 6 tea light candles or wax pellets
- A pillar candle that is thinner than your candle jar
- Flowers of your choice
- Essential oil (optional)

Directions:

1. Choose your glass candle jar.
2. Check to see your pillar candle is the right width and height. You should have at least 1-2cm gap in between the glass and the candle. If the candle is too tall, shave off some wax from the bottom of the candle using a hot knife. The very top of the candle should sit just above the lip of the glass.
3. Place your flowers in between the candle and pillar. You can use any flower you like – I used lavender but you could also use rose petals, or herbs such as rosemary. Make sure the glass is quite tightly packed with flowers as many of them will be covered by wax.
4. I used shaved down tea light candles with the wick removed for my wax, but you can also buy wax pellets from craft stores if you wish. Place your wax in a heat proof jar (a jam jar works well!). Heat water in a saucepan until it's gently boiling, and carefully place the jar in the middle. Let it melt slowly over a low setting.
5. When your wax is completely melted, carefully remove the jar from the saucepan with a cloth. At this point, you can add essential oils if you wish.
6. Pour the melted wax over your flowers. Tap the glass to make sure there are no air bubbles. The wax should reach just under the lip of the glass. If you don't have enough, melt more wax.

34

DIY Survival Candle

DIY survival candles are valuable items especially in times of emergency, such as disasters and floods. Candles sold in the market and online can be very expensive and only last for a short period of time. It is for this very reason why many preppers choose to make "survival candles" at home using less expensive higher quality materials.

What you'll need:

- Soy Wax Flakes
- Canning Jars
- Wick and Tabs
- Scissors
- Double Boiler
- A pouring device
- Protective Gloves

Directions:

1. Get the wicks ready. Make sure to measure them against the container or jar to be used. Then, trim them down if they are way too long.
2. Put the wicks in the jars. Do not worry if wicks are not centered. They can be fixed while pouring the wax.
3. Melt the wax. Fill the larger pot with water. Allow it to boil. Next, insert a smaller pot inside and put the wax flakes onto the smaller pot.
4. Carefully transfer the melted wax onto the container. Do not fill the jar up the whole way, leave some space between the wax and the top of the jar. While pouring the wax, one can also adjust the wick so that it goes into the center of the jar.
5. Trim the wick as needed. After the wax has cooled down, trim the wick as needed. It should only be at least ¼" from the wax.

35

DIY Gel Candle

Basic Gel Candles are easy to make and attract everyone's attention with the vibrant colors and translucent gel!

What you'll need:

- Candle Gel Wax
- A melting pot for wax
- Pre-tabbed wicks
- A thermometer
- Liquid candle dye

- Scent
- A stove or hot plate
- A suitable work area
- Glass jars to pour your gel into

Directions:

1. Prepare your work area – gather your materials. Place your gel into an electric melting pot, with a temperature control or directly on you stove burner on med/low heat.

2. Heat to 250 F and keep it at this temperature until the gel appears as a clear liquid. Attach your wick tab to the bottom center of the container either with hot glue or a small piece of double back tape or a dot of melted gel.

3. Add your color and fragrance, stir well, stir some more, and then keep stirring. By stirring and mixing you are making absolutely sure that the fragrance mixes with the gel properly so that your candles will not cloud or appear distorted when they are cool. Only a very small amount of liquid dye is needed to color your gel.

   NOTE: You must use a liquid candle dye. You cannot use powered or wax dye chips. Please remember that adding more than the recommended amount of fragrance to your gel creates a fire hazard.

4. Allow the gel to cool to 200 F. Pour your candle between 180 F and 200 F.

5. Enjoy your candles! Watch them burn and enjoy the fragrance that you picked. Handmade candles also make great gifts. Your friends will enjoy receiving something that's handmade and if the directions are followed properly you will have made candles that are a better quality than what you can buy in most stores!

36

DIY Grapefruit Fir Candle

If you're like us and prefer pretty looking things but have no money to spend on them, consider making your own candles. It is way easier than we anticipated and actually a lot of fun. We seem to hoard essential oils so it was fun to go through our stash and pair up scents that we thought would work together. We opted for grapefruit and fir because it's the ultimate Spring mix. Fir is clearly a Winter scent, while grapefruit tends to remind us of Summer. You can absolutely use one scent or mix as many as you'd like. Go crazy!

What you'll need:

- Soy Wax Flakes
- Natural Candle Wicks
- Grapefruit Essential Oil
- Fir Needle Essential Oil
- Saucepan (Use one that can be dedicated to candle making)
- Pencils
- Old-Fashioned Glasses

Directions:

1. 1. Lay parchment/wax paper down next to your stove to make clean-up easier.
2. 2. Measure out your wax flakes. A good rule of thumb is to double the volume of each candle vessel.
3. 3. Hot glue the metal wick plates to the bottom of each vessel, then wrap the excess wick around a pencil and rest on the opening.
4. 4. Heat the wax on low heat, stirring frequently just until the wax flakes are melted. Remove the pan from heat.
5. 5. Add roughly 20 drops of each essential oil per candle to the pan and give it a stir. (The number of drops you'll need will greatly depend on how strong you'd like the scent to be and the brand of essential oil you use.) Since I'm making 2 candles, I've added 40 drops of each oil.
6. 6. Next, evenly divide the wax between the vessels and allow to cool to a solid state.
7. 7. Once the wax is completely cool, trim the wicks to ½".

37

DIY Valentines Day Candle

The greeting card companies want you to believe that valentine's day is about the chocolates, and diamonds and whatever else expensive things you buy... but really, this is one of the holidays where it's definitely the thought that counts.

What you'll need:

- A Mason Jar with lid
- Rubbing Alcohol and paper towels
- Chalk paint
- Contact paper
- White paint pen
- Sharpie
- Scissors
- Paint brush
- Hammer and a nail

Direction:

1. Clean your mason jar with rubbing alcohol and paper towels. You want a clean surface to start with.
2. Trace or draw a heart on contact paper with your sharpie
3. Now take your handy dandy scissors and cut that sucker out.
4. Stick your heart on the jar. We're going to use it to create negative space.
5. Ready, set, PAINT!

    While you're waiting for it to dry (and not letting your cat eat it or leave prints... just me? moving on) you can work on the lid.

6. Trace whatever shape you like on the lid. You're going to use the hammer and nail to punch holes in it to make your shape so KISS (Keep It Simple Stupid)
7. Yep, use the hammer and nail to punch holes along your shape about 1/2 centimeter apart.

8. Use the rubbing alcohol to get the outline off of your lid and voila! You made a punch lid with the best of them.

9. Now that your jar should be dry, peel the contact paper heart off and admire your handiwork.

10. Take the paint pen and make polkadots and notes, or whatever to your hearts content. I just went for a dotted line around the window.

11. Fill the jar with your worksheet strips and/or a votive candle and give it to your sweet heart. Or keep it yourself, because like me, you are single and deserve to give yourself something nice.

38

DIY Pumpkin Spice Candle

Anyone who has ever been to my house knows that I almost always have a candle burning. With a house full of boys, sometimes there are not-so-great smells lingering in the air that just need to GO! Candles are a quick solution for those yucky boy smells and they work fast, which is why I love them so much. Within a few minutes of lighting them, the smell is usually gone.

What you'll need:

- 2 cups soy wax flakes
- 1 Tablespoon liquid vanilla candle scent
- 1 Tablespoon pumpkin pie spice

- Long waxed candle wick
- 8oz Mason jar
- Long wooden skewer or pencil
- Glass measuring cup

Directions:

1. Place 2 cups of your wax flakes in your glass measuring cup and heat in the microwave for about two minutes or till completely melted (careful this will be very hot).
2. Dip the bottom metal part of your candlewick into the wax and press on into the bottom center of your mason jar and wrap the top of the wick around your wooden skewer and place across the top of the jar.
3. Now use a potholder to carefully remove the hot wax from your microwave.
4. Mix in your vanilla scent and pumpkin spice.
5. Now use a potholder again to carefully pour the hot wax into your mason jar.
6. Use your potholder to transfer your filled Mason jar to the freezer and freeze for about an hour.
7. Trim the top of the wick and light.

39

DIY Beeswax Candle in Mason Jar

These DIY Beeswax Candles create invigorating aroma- beeswax and lemon is so refreshing! For this DIY we will use Clear Glass Mason Jars. If you are using these jars for canning they come in 2 sizes and also have a 2 piece silver plastisol lined canning lid. The plastisol liner is activated by heat to create a tamper evident hermetic seal… perfect for jams and other treats!

What you'll need:

- Clear Glass Mason Jars
- Cotton candle wick with tabs – about 8" pieces

- 1 pound Beeswax (found at your local craft store)
- 1/2 cup Coconut Oil
- 20 drops of lemon essential oil
- Old 2 cup glass measuring cup (that you don't mind wax getting on)
- Lemon zest
- Large saucepan to boil water
- Hammer and screwdriver to break up beeswax
- Clothespins to hold the wick in place
- Wooden skewer for stirring

Directions:

1. Using the hammer and screwdriver break off chunks of your beeswax. This helps the beeswax to melt faster. For easy cleanup of any wax that remains on the screwdriver just dip it in the boiling water and then carefully wipe clean with a paper towel.

2. Add the beeswax chunks (1 pound worth) and the 1/2 cup coconut oil to the glass measuring cup and carefully place in the boiling water. It will take a while for the beeswax to melt but it will happen! Use the skewer to stir to make sure every little bit melts.

3. Once all melted you can now add about 20 drops of lemon essential oil.

4. CAREFULLY pour a little bit of the wax into the bottom of your glass mason jar, about 1/2 inch worth. Using a skewer push the tabs that are attached to the cotton wick to the bottom of the mason jar and hold in place with the skewer while the wax hardens for minute. For this size jar, use 2 wicks.

5. Clip clothespins onto the top of the wick and balance the clothespins on the edge of the jar. This will help keep the wick from falling into the candle while the rest of the wax hardens.

6. Finish pouring the rest of your wax into the jar. Fill all the way to the top. At this point don't move your jars until they are completely cool. As the top starts to get hard you can zest some lemon zest for decoration.

7. Let cool completely then trim your wax to about 1/4"!

40

Eucalyptus Essential Oil Candle

Burning soy candles not only smells great, but soy candles burn clean and last so much longer as well. One of the most recent candles we made is this fantastic eucalyptus essential oil candle, perfect for burning year round and reaping all the benefits of eucalyptus oil from!

Want to make your own? You don't need any fancy equipment.

What you'll need:

- 16 oz. canning jars
- 2 1/2 cups of soy candle flakes
- 1 green crayon
- 6 inch or more candle wick w/ weighted base
- Pencil or chopstick
- 10-15 drops of Eucalyptus Essential Oil

Directions:

1. Begin by heating the soy flakes on a medium heat in a teflon pan. Keep the flakes moving to avoid sticking or clumping.

2. Once the flakes are liquid, lower the heat and drop in broken pieces of crayon into the liquid. Continue to stir so the color distributes. Remove from heat and set aside. This is when you can stir in the drops of eucalyptus essential oil. Smells amazing, right?

3. Now, wrap the ends of the wick on a pencil or chopstick. Allow the weight to drop to the bottom of the jar and use the stick to hold the wick in place at the top.

4. Slowly pour the melted soy flakes into the jar. Adjust the wick if needed because you want it to stay centered. Right now, it will look like a wick soaking in Ecto Cooler!

5. Set the jar in a cool place where it can have the time to harden. This will take on average 4 hours. Do not disturb it prior to this four hour period. While it may look solid, the inside of the candle could be soft still. Avoid touching, shaking, or fussing with it.

6. You can now take scissors and cut the wick down so it is about 1/2 an inch in length. It is now ready to be lit and of course, enjoyed. Remember to be a responsible candle owner, my friends. Never burn candles unattended!

41

DIY Sea Shell Candle

These small tea lights holders are perfect beach theme table decor. I had seen them on Pinterest and got inspired.

What you'll need:

- Oyster Shell
- Wicks

- Centering Device
- Soy Candle Wax
- A Stainless Steel Pot (to melt the wax)

Directions:

1. Cut the wicks to 1 1/2 inch length. Use the centering device to center the wick. This device will hold it firmly in the oyster shell.
2. You will need 1 lb of soy wax which will make about small 25 oyster shell tea lights. Each oyster shell holds 2 tbsp of wax.
3. The pot you use should be designated for candle making, so don't pick anything that you use every day. It's tough to remove wax from the bottom of a pot. Check out flea market for used stainless steel pots.
4. Measure 1 cup at a time into the pot and place on the burner. The wax will melt in minutes. It only takes 15 minutes for the wax to harden.

42

DIY No Wax Candle

Make a candle at home with no wax. It burns for 40 hours and will make your apartment smell amazing!

What you'll need:

- Jar
- Vegetable Shortening
- Crayons

- Scented Essential Oil
- 100% Cotton String
- Scissors
- Nut (hardware)
- Skewer Stick

Directions:

1. Clean and dry a clear jar to hold the candle in
2. Fill jar with vegetable shortening and leave about 1 inch of space at the top
3. Microwave the jar for 2 minutes to melt the vegetable shortening
4. Melt crayons in the microwave, pour in the jar, and mix to add color to the candle
5. Add a tablespoon of scented essential oil
6. Cut about 1 foot of the cotton string
7. Tie one end of the string to a nut
8. Drop the nut in the center of the jar and loop string around the skewer to set the wick
9. Freeze for thirty minutes
10. Cut string to leave about 1/4 inch of the string for the wick

43

Dried Flower Candles

Embed flowers onto a candle by affixing dried flowers to the surface, then over-dipping in clear wax. This technique works especially well with interestingly shaped leaves and flat blooms.

What you'll need:

- 2 pounds kitty litter
- Fresh or dried flowers, such as pansies and violets
- 1 Basic Recipe Molded Candle

- Stick-um or other craft adhesive
- 1.5 pound dip-and-carve or paraffin wax

Directions:

1. If using fresh flowers, cover a cookie sheet with a layer of kitty litter and place the flowers and leaves on top. Sprinkle enough kitty litter over the flowers to completely cover. Leave to dry in a cool, dry place (where kitty can't get at them!) for at least a week. (Silicone beads work similarly, but will dry the flowers in 24 to 48 hours.)
2. Carefully remove the flowers from the litter and lay them out in a pleasing arrangement on a sheet of paper.
3. Use a dab of Stick-um to affix the flowers to the candle. Do this to each flower until the arrangement is complete, making sure the flowers remain flat against the candle.
4. In a 9-inch dipping can, set in the bottom of a double boiler over medium heat, melt the wax. Heat to 205 degrees Fahrenheit. (Be extra vigilant at these temperatures.)
5. Holding the candle by the wick, carefully dip it in the wax. Hold for 5 seconds. Remove and make sure the flowers are flat.
6. Dip again for 5 seconds. Remove and leave to dry for 2 hours. Trim the wick to 1/4 inch and you are ready to light your candle.

44

DIY Floral Candle

These DIY Floral Candles are the perfect Valentine's Day gift or you might even decide to keep them for yourself ;)

What you'll need:

- Metal Tins
- Red Gingham Washi Tape

- White Jute Cord
- Kraft Tags
- Soy Candle Wax Flakes
- Wood Candle Wicks
- Hot Glue Gun
- Empty Aluminum Can
- Tongs
- Fresh Flowers
- Essential oils (Optional)

Directions:

1. Begin by filling an empty aluminum can with the Wax Flakes. Place it in a pot of water and heat the water to boiling and then reduce to a simmer until the wax it completely melted. It will end up looking like olive oil.

2. While the wax is melting prepare your metal tin containers by hot gluing the wick to the bottom so they stay put while pouring the melted wax.

3. Once the wax is melted, using tongs (because it will be really hot), pour the wax into the metal tins, and then add in a few petals from your fresh flowers.

4. Let that harden, and then add more fresh flowers and just barely cover them with more wax. Essentially you are creating layers of wax with fresh flower petals mixed in. I also added about 6 drops of lavender essential oil at this point to give it a nice smell, but this is optional.

5. Do this 2 or 3 times until you have the wax almost to the top of the wick. Use different types of flowers for different looks.

    After the candles have hardened you are ready to give them away! (Or keep them).

45

DIY Beeswax Tea Light Candle

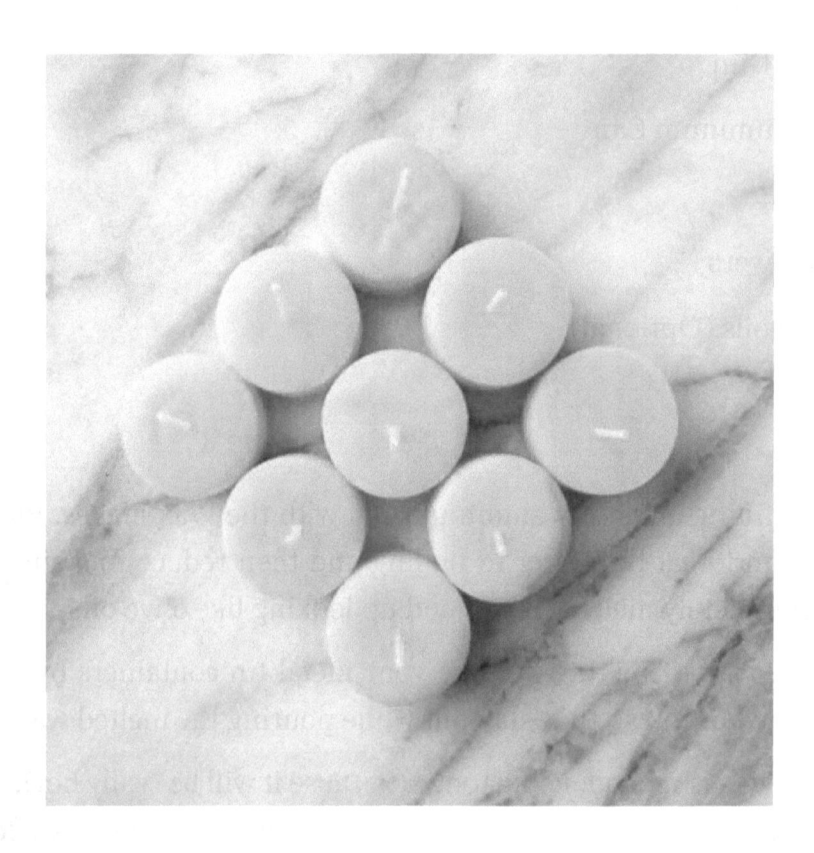

There is something so peaceful about working with this gorgeous bit of creation and they really are quite simple to make. I love knowing that I can make inexpensively beautiful and healthy candles for my home.

What you'll need:

- Beeswax
- Wick

- Hairpins
- Scissors
- Small muffin tin (I use a 24 tin)
- Tin Can
- Newspaper

Directions:

1. Layer your area well with newspaper. Of course the idea is to avoid any spillage but this is essential because it makes cleanup a breeze.
2. Place your beeswax in a tin can and warm in the oven at 180 F. Don't heat it higher than this because it will burn the wax. I usually place a piece of tinfoil under the can to make sure that no drips get in the oven.
3. Prep your muffin tin with wicks.
4. Once the wax has melted, dip each wick to the height you want the candle to be. Mine are about 3/4 inch thick. Straighten each wick as you dip it and lay the hair pin across each muffin cup, centering it.
5. When you have the muffin tin prepped with the wicks, pour the wax into each cup. The beeswax hardens fast so it is important to work quickly and carefully.
6. Allow the candles to cure by leaving them to harden for at least an hour. Remove the hair pin and they should quite easily pop out. Trim the wicks if needed.

46

DIY Spiced Beeswax Autumn Candle

Beeswax candles are unique in that they actually release healthy ions into the air, creating a healthier environment. Enjoy pouring just one candle for the house or an entire batch for a super-sweet gift.

What you'll need:

- 100% organic beeswax pellets (or a block, chopped into small shavings)
- Organic virgin cold-pressed coconut oil
- 1/8 tsp organic clove, ground

- 1/8 tsp organic cinnamon, ground
- 1/8 tsp organic nutmeg, ground
- 1 tbsp christmas-tree trimmings, minced, or cedar, minced
- 1 ceramic or glass jar (any recycled glass container in your house will do)
- Cotton wick
- Chopsticks
- Knife for stirring
- Large pyrex measuring cup
- Medium sized pot

Directions:

1. Coat your Pyrex measuring cup and knife with coconut oil to make cleaning the items easier. Fill your pot with three inches of water and bring to a medium-high boil. Measure your beeswax in your chosen jar. In order to get one candle, you'll need about 1 and 1/2 of your jar.

2. Place your measured beeswax into your Pyrex. Place your Pyrex into the boiling water to create a double boiler so your wax will melt smoothly and evenly. This process will take about 15-30 minutes depending on the size of jar you've chosen.

3. While wax is melting, add your spices and tree trimmings to a separate small bowl and mix together well.

4. Place your wick into your chosen glass and secure it in the middle with two chopsticks (odd, but these will hold your wick intact while pouring in your wax).

5. Now that your wax is melted, carefully remove your Pyrex from the boiling water and add spice and trimming mix to melted wax. Use your knife to stir wax and mix until no clumps from the spices remain.

6. Slowly pour your wax, spice, and trimming mix into your glass slowly, as not to disturb the wick.

7. Let your candle set for about thirty minutes. Trim wick and enjoy the magic illumination of your new candle.

47

DIY Marbled Easter Egg Candles

Try these simple Marbleized Egg Shell Candles this Easter to spice up your spring home decor.

What you'll need:

- Egg Shells
- Nail Polish
- Old Candle and Wick

Directions:

1. Make sure you don't crack open the entire egg shell. Open only the top portion for the candle to burn. And wash them. Drop the nail polish in the water, I have splattered them in the bowl of water

2. Drop the nail polish in the water, I have splattered them in the bowl of water, you can marbleize however you want them to be.

3. Time to melt the wax! I collected all the tiny floating candles leftovers and melted them.

4. Now, pour the wax into the egg shell. The shell is going to be very hot after you pour the wax, so avoid touching them immediately. Let them cool.

48

DIY Ombre Candle

I absolutely love the dip-dyed/ombre look! Recently I've been looking for projects that feature this trend. I came across this easy technique and used it to upcycle extra white candles that I had around the house. This is a thrifty way to add a pop of color to a party or wedding… buy plain candles in bulk and dye them to match any decor!

What you'll need:

- White candles (pillar, taper, or votive)
- Old candle wax or scentsy bars

- Crayons (for dyeing white candle wax)
- Can or glass jar
- Wooden stirrer

Directions:

1. Separate old candles or scentsy bars by color (I used a mixture of pink and red). If you're working with leftover white candle wax, choose a crayon to dye the wax. Place chunks of wax (along with bits of crayon, if needed) into a glass jar or can.
2. Fill a small saucepan with several inches of water. Place can of wax into saucepan. Warm over a burner on low heat. Gently stir wax as it melts (be careful not to get any water into the wax).
3. When wax has fully melted, remove can from saucepan (be cautious, it'll be hot!).
4. Take a candle and dip halfway into the wax (dip quickly to achieve a very light layer of wax), this will be the lightest level. Continue this process, dipping less of the candle in each time. Place finished candles on a piece of parchment paper to dry.

The best part about this project? I didn't have to buy a thing for it! This is a great way to recycle extra candles into a fresh accessory for your home!

49

DIY Mug Candle

Candle making is one of my favorite hobbies. They're quick and simple to make, and the possibilities are endless. I enjoy making soy candles to give for the holidays, birthdays and Mother's Day. They make lovely gifts, especially in gift baskets, and very easy to make with a few simple supplies.

What you'll need:

- Soy wax flakes
- Campfire mug
- Wood wick

- Large Pyrex cup or wax melting pot
- Hot glue
- Fragrance oil set

Directions:

1. To make a campfire mug candle you will need 3 cups of soy wax flakes per candle.
2. Begin by gluing the wick to the center of the mug; firmly hold in place until glue is set.
3. Use a candle wax melting pot over a double boiler to melt soy wax. Candle wax can also be melted in the microwave using a large Pyrex glass cup; stirring every 30 seconds until melted.
4. Remove melted wax from heat and allow to cool for 5-10 minutes before adding fragrance oil.
5. Stir in 15-20 drops fragrance oil into melted wax, then pour into mug.
6. Allow candle to set for a few hours, preferably overnight.
7. Trim wick to ¼ inch before lighting.
8. Always use caution when burning candles and trim wick if needed.

50

DIY Soy Wax Candle

Soy wax is a much cleaner alternative to synthetic paraffin wax. The soy wax burns cleaner and does not release any toxins into the air. It also burns at a lower temperature, so the candles will last you longer than if you were burning regular paraffin wax.

What you'll need:

- Wide mouth mason jars

- Candle wicks with metal tabs
- Container soy wax (8 cups of flaked wax = 4 cups of melted wax)
- Essential oils of your choice

Directions:

1. Start by glueing your wix (with tabs) to the bottom of the containers.
2. Simmer 1-2 inches of water in a medium pot on the stove.
3. Place wax in a double broiler or pyrex glass and slowly melt, making sure to stir occasionally. Once all the wax has melted down, take off the heat.
4. Let wax cool to approximately 120 degrees farenheit (I use a meat thermometer for this). Add essential oils at this point and pour into containers.
5. Let cool till solid (overnight) and then trim the wix.

51

DIY Forest Pine Candle

Envelop your senses and create magical ambience with the delightful smell of nature, reminiscent of an evening romp through the Northern forest. Pine Forest will absolutely enchant you with its clean and energizing aroma. Woodsy, sweet and warm, this smooth scent of Pine is a relaxant, good for anxiety and calming the mind and senses.

What you'll need:

- Soy wax flakes

- Forest Pine fragrance (I LOVE this holiday fragrance set!)
- Glass jar with lid
- Gold Spray paint – (this is my Hands Down FAVORITE gold spray paint!)
- Candle wick
- Hot glue gun and hot glue

Directions:

1. Spray paint lid of glass jar with one or two coats of gold spray paint. Let dry between each coat. I'm in love with this spray paint line and this gold color – it's high quality and sprays on like a dream! I can't wait to try out their silver color too!
2. Glue a wick to the center bottom of the jar.
3. Melt soy wax flakes in a large microwave-safe bowl for a minute or 2. 4 cups of wax will fill fit one mid-size and one small jar. You can always melt more if needed. I use a large pyrex measuring cup for pouring. (Use the double boiler method instead of the microwave to melt the wax if you like. Stir every 30 seconds until wax is completely melted.)
4. Stir in about 15 drops of fragrance oil into melted wax or more until scented to the way you like it.
5. Pour wax slowly into jar and let the candle sit for several hours or overnight until solid.
6. Once the candle is solid, trim wick to ¼ inch. Once candle has completely cooled add lid.

52

DIY Tin Punched Votive Candle

I have absurdly fond memories of childhood crafts. Paper bag puppets, woven baskets, pop-up cards, and yes, even colorful beans glued to a paint-stirrer in the name of a Mother's Day gift for my poor mom. My heart raced with each craft I made. But perhaps my favorite craft was taught to me by my third grade teacher, Mrs. Kendall. She brought in canning jar lids and templates and allowed us to tin-punch ornaments as Christmas gifts for our parents. I loved it!

What you'll need:

- Tin can (opened and emptied)

- Primer
- Gold and white spray paint (or multi-surface acrylic paint)
- Rice
- Water
- Tape (preferably duct tape)
- Printed template (i simply printed out large letters to spell a word, though you can find lots of tin-punch patterns with a quick internet search.)
- Mallet or hammer
- Punch or nail
- Brush (if not using spray paint)

Directions:

1. Remove the labels and adhesive from the cans, thoroughly clean each can, then dry completely. I removed the label adhesive with a mixture of olive oil and baking soda.
2. Fill each can with rice and water to the top. Freeze completely. This will provide a stable can for punching, preventing the can from denting or collapsing.
3. Tape a printed template onto the can by wrapping the can with duct tape. The tape will not stick to a frozen can, but the tape will stick to the paper—hence the wrapping of the can. Use a punch tool or nail to hammer nail-sized holes along the border of the template.
4. Make sure the holes are at least the diameter of a standard nail, or the light will not properly show through the finished candle holders.

53

DIY Sea Glass Candle

Sea glass or beach glass candles are a nice and fairly simple way to make a beach craft project using your sea glass collection.

What you'll need:

- A glass vase, goblet, or other container about the size pictured here.
- A candle
- Sand

- Sea Glass or Beach Glass. (try beach glass of all one color or mix a combination of colors).

Directions:

1. Center the candle in the middle of the goblet.
2. Fill about 1/3 with sand, making sure the candle is centered.
3. Then, fill the rest with your jewelry or craft grade sea glass.
4. Alternately, you could use seashells and small pieces of driftwood or pebbles to contrast with your seaglass.

54

Coffee Scented Candles

I am such a fan of coffee scented candles. This easy tutorial for Coffee Scented Candles is a great choice for a fun and unique gift idea. Give them as gifts to any coffee lover or use them to scent your home! The tutorial uses soy wax flakes and real coffee grounds.

What you'll need:

- 2 cups of soy wax flakes
- 1 candle wick w/weighted bottom
- 1 teaspoon of coffee grounds (I used dry, unused grounds from a K-cup.)

- Chopstick, wood stick, or pencil
- 1 brown or tan crayon
- Container

Directions:

1. Start by heating up the soy wax flakes on a low heat. You want to use a non-stick pot and stir often as it heats up.
2. You can now tint the wax to add color. DO NOT use food coloring as it won't mix. Instead, take a brown or tan crayon, peel it, and drop the broken pieces into the wax mixture. Stir well.
3. Prepare to set the wick by wrapping it around a pencil or chopstick.
4. Set the stick over the cup and let the weight of the wick drop to the bottom of the container.
5. Take the mixture from heat and pour it into the jar. You can re-center the wick should it shift.
6. Take half of your coffee grounds and sprinkle them into the mixture. Reserve the rest.
7. Set the candle in a cool spot. Allow it to harden. About 30 minutes in when it has started to solidify, sprinkle the top of the candle with the remaining coffee grounds.
8. Once the candle has hardened (may take up to 4 hours) just snip the wick to shorten it. Light your candle and enjoy.

55

DIY Poured Herbal Candle

Creating hand poured herbal candles with a few key ingredients can bring the outdoors in and allow us to skip the chemicals. Candles are uniquely relaxing, and with the addition of herbs and essential oils, become an aromatherapeutic experience.

What you'll need:

- 2 2-ounce metal candle tins
- 4 ounces soy wax flakes

- 2 small wood wicks and clips
- 2 glue dots
- 12 drops German chamomile essential oil (Matricaria chamomilla)
- 12 drops neroli essential oil (Citrus aurantium)
- 1 teaspoon dried chamomile flowers

Directions:

1. Using glue dots, adhere wood wick clips to the center base of each candle tin. Insert wood wicks, cut the wicks right at the top of each tin, and set aside.
2. Fill a large saucepan with about 2 inches of water and place it on the stove to heat. Place soy wax flakes in a metal candle pouring pitcher and set inside the large saucepan.
3. Whisk often and heat until melted using the double broiler method. Remove from heat immediately to avoid wax becoming too hot. Let the wax cool to 120°F to 125°F before adding essential oils.
4. Once the wax has cooled, add essential oils and whisk or swirl to combine. Carefully pour scented soy wax into prepared candle tins.
5. Sprinkle dried herbs on the top of each candle. Let cool 30 minutes to 1 hour or until wax is hard and white.
6. Always burn soy candles long enough for the wax to melt across the container before blowing out the flame to avoid formation of a tunnel in the wax, which will shorten the life of the candle.

56

Lemon Beeswax Candle

Beeswax releases negative ions when burned. Positive ions in the air include bacteria, allergens, viruses, dust, and pollen. Opposites attract. What that means is that the negative ions from beeswax attach to the positive toxins in the air. The attached particles become heavier, and are pulled down to the ground and out of the air where you'd breathe them. Kind of amazing, right?

What you'll need:

- Organic beeswax (make certain it is 100% otherwise it could contain petroleum based wax as well)

- Lemons (or the heat safe container of your choice)
- Wooden wicks
- Newspaper to cover work area
- Double boiler

Directions:

1. I poured my beeswax into lemon peels, offering a subtle citrus scent to the sweet smell of honey. If you're pouring your wax into a glass jar or container, add a bit of coconut oil to the melted beeswax before pouring.
2. Break your block of beeswax into pieces and place in a glass bowl over a pan filled with simmering water. Melt over medium heat.
3. While your wax is melting, prepare your lemons! Slice in half and carefully insert a knife around the edge to separate the fruit from the peel.
4. Once the wax begins to melt, cut your wicks and dip the ends in to coat the base of your wick with enough wax to adhere it to the bottom of your lemons.
5. If you'd like to add an all-natural scent or citronella oil to your candles, stir it into your melted wax. Here's when you'd add your coconut oil if you're using glass containers.
6. When your beeswax is entirely melted, pour into each lemon. Hold the wick steady while you're pouring and until the wax is hardened enough for the wick to stand on its own. Repeat with each of your lemons.
7. Trim the wicks, and breathe easy. These little homemade beauties are making things lemony and lovely, all while purifying your air.

57

DIY Tissue Paper Candle

Have you ever thought about making your own candles? These tissue paper candles are a great way to personalize your home with something unique.

What you'll need:

- Tissue paper
- Images

- Inkjet printer
- Craft knife or scissors
- Wax paper
- Hairdryer

Directions:

1. Print the image on tissue paper, making sure the paper feeds through the printer correctly.
2. Leave to dry completely then cut around the edges with a craft knife or scissors. Leave a 2-mm border around the edges of the image.
3. Position the image onto the candle and cover the image with a piece of wax paper big enough to wrap around the entire candle.
4. Lift the candle up by holding the edges of the wax paper together at the back of the candle.
5. Hold the hairdryer approximately 2 cm from the candle. Blow heat onto the tissue paper images, covering the whole image.
6. The wax will start to melt and bleed into the tissue paper. Carefully peel back the wax paper.

58

DIY Starbucks Candle

Okay, this is truly a one of a kind, unique candle. This is a handmade, coffee scented, soy wax candle poured in a re-purposed glass Starbucks ice coffee container. It's really a work of art.

What you'll need:

- Wax (soy wax or reused candle wax)
- Red color pigment or red crayons

- Mini paper cups
- Candle wicks

Directions:

1. Use a hot glue gun to attach the wick to the bottom of the paper cup. To keep the candle wick upright and centered, tape some scotch tape over the center of the cup opening.

2. Time to melt the wax! Microwave your wax a minute per cup. After the wax is fully melted, add in the color pigments and the fragrance oils.

3. Pour the mixture into your paper cups, and let the wax sit for an hour.

4. To make the whipped cream, slightly melt some white wax. Don't melt it completely because you want it to keep a chunky texture so that it looks like realistic whipped cream. Make sure the red wax in the cups are fully hardened, and then place the "whipped cream" wax onto the candle cups.

5. To get the drizzled caramel sauce, melt an orange-brown crayon over the candle and let it drip over the wax. Peel the paper cup off the candle. Print out the Starbucks logo, cut it out, and glue it onto your candle. And you're done! Enjoy!

59

DIY Hidden Gem Candle

Get some good vibes in your space by burning these DIY hidden crystal candles. (And make lots of extras to give as gifts too!)

What you'll need:

- 16 ounces soy wax
- Cotton candle wicks

- 6-8 ounce glass jars
- Healing crystals
- Gloss Mod Podge
- Food coloring
- Sweet orange, clove and ginger essential oils

Directions:

1. Combine 1 tablespoon gloss Mod Podge with 1 teaspoon water in a small cup.
2. Add food coloring one drop at a time until you get the perfect color (once baked the color will look a lot lighter than when you started so don't be afraid to go a little dark).
3. When you have a color you like, pour the mixture into the jar and swirl it around until the inside is completely coated.
4. Pour out any excess, set the jars upside down on a lined baking tray and let dry for at least 45 minutes. Then bake at 225°F for 1 hour.
5. After the jars have cooled, slowly melt the soy wax chips (I melt mine in an old 16-ounce glass jar in the microwave, checking often).
6. Secure the wick to the bottom of the jar and carefully place your crystal next to the wick. Once the wax is completely melted add essential oils and stir.
7. Then pour into the jar and let it sit until the wax hardens. Trim wick if needed.

60

Wood Wick Teacup Candles

There is nothing that adds a fun vintage flair to a shower quite like these teacup candles. And they are so versatile! I will be using them for a Beauty and the Beast themed bridal shower, but they could just as easily be used for a tea party, Jane Austen Shower, or Mother's Day Brunch!

What you'll need:

- Mismatched teacups and saucers
- Wooden candle wicks
- Candle wax

- Candle pouring pot
- Powdered candle dye
- Essential oils for scent

Directions:

1. Melt wax on low heat in your pot. If, like me, you are using candle stubs, remove the wicks from the old candles once the wax is completely melted using either tongs or a fork.
2. For these candles, the full wax wick is far too long. Insert the wood wick into its metal stand and place in the cup. Cut the wicks at the top of the teacup with a pair of scissors, then remove the candle wax from heat and soak them in the wax for 10 minutes.
3. Once wicks have been soaked, remove them with tongs or a fork. Once they are cool enough to handle (I was able to touch them immediately) insert them into the metal holder stands included and let dry.
4. Now, attach the wicks to the bottom of your teacups by dipping the metal holder into the melted wax, then position at the bottom of the jar.
5. Let the wax cool for a couple more minutes, then add color and fragrance of your choice.
6. Pour cooled (but still liquid) wax into the teacups. Reserve about 25% of your wax to remelt and top off your candles if a divot is created in the middle due to the wax cooling.
7. Once candles are cooled and solidified, remelt the excess wax and fill in any divots that were caused during the first pour. Now you have a lovely set of candles for your home or favors for your next party!

61

DIY Floating Halloween Candle

There are two reasons I'm featuring yet another Halloween project (previous one being the Animal Eyes Wreath from a week ago) when it's only the first week in September. One, because like most of you, I'm absolutely crazy about all things surrounding Autumn and Halloween!

What you'll need:

- Cardboard tubes

- High temp glue gun
- High temp glue sticks
- Spray paint (antique white)
- Flickering led tea lights
- Black thread or suction cups

Directions:

1. Using scissors cut the end of a tube to resemble the uneven edges of a candle.
2. Use a scrap piece of Styrofoam or a ball of wadded up newspaper wedged into the cut end to make a base for the tea light to rest on.
3. Apply glue to edge of "candlestick," allowing for varying lengths of "wax drips." Hold the glue gun in place through multiple pumps for extra-long drips.
4. Cover entire candle with multiple coats of antique white spray paint. If you've got more time on your hands (or don't have two crazy little boys running around!), you can always cover the diagonal lines of the tube with a thin coat of paper mache.
5. Candles Hanging With Thread: Using a needle and black thread, tie a loop just above the candle base. I tried both fishing wire and black thread. Black thread definitely worked better! The fishing wire looked good during the day but, as you can see in my ridiculously grainy picture below, reflected the glow from the tea light at night.
6. Halloween Candles Suspended With Window Hooks: If you're using these inside and in front of a window, this is the way to go! Just puncture a hole in the tube large enough for the hook to fit in and suction to a window. Make sure you get suction hooks small enough to be hidden by the Halloween candles.

Now, what are you waiting for...start hoarding those tubes and get to make these fun floating Halloween candles. You'll be oh so happy you did come Halloween night!

62

DIY Gilded Birthday Candle

Two light coats is all you need and voila, beautiful gilded birthday candles.

What you'll need:

- Gold spray paint (I used this)
- Birthday candles
- Newspaper/cardboard

Directions:

1. Lay desired number of candles on newspaper (or whatever surface you decided to spray paint on). Holding the spray paint 4-5 inches away from candles, spray until fully coated.
2. Let dry for 15-20 minutes, roll over and repeat.
3. Spray both sides twice and let them dry fully before use.
4. Decorate your favorite cake, make a wish.

63

DIY Metallic Colored Candle

Making homemade candles is a creative and relaxing hobby with endless possibilities. The variety of colors, scents and designs available to the candle hobbyist are myriad. Typically, candle dyes are mixed with the wax to color the candle throughout. Metallic dyes, however, cannot be mixed directly with candle wax; the metallic flakes will clog the wicks and the candles will not burn well. Metallic dyes should be used only to coat candles. Learn the dipping method and fill your home with lovely candles in shimmery shades of gold, silver, bronze and copper.

What you'll need:

- Large double boiler
- Paraffin wax
- Metallic pigment dye
- White or ivory candles
- Wax paper
- Clothesline

Directions:

1. Fill the bottom pot of your double boiler two-thirds full with water. Bring to a boil, then reduce to a simmer.

2. Pour 2 lbs. chopped paraffin wax into the top pot of your double boiler. Place the top pot on the bottom pot to melt the paraffin wax. Stir occasionally for even melting.

3. Add approximately 2/3 oz. of pigment dye to the melting paraffin wax. The amount of pigment dye needed to color the wax may vary slightly depending on the product; follow the manufacturer's instructions.

4. Stir the paraffin wax and pigment dye together until thoroughly melted and blended.

5. Hold your white or ivory candles by the wicks and dip them into the melted wax. Cover them completely, but do not allow the colored wax to cover the wicks or seep into the wick wells. Place the candles on wax paper to dry, or, if they will not stand, hang them from a clothesline by their wicks with clothespins.

6. Repeat Step 5 until you have achieved your desired color. Remember to let your candles dry between each dip.

64

DIY Color Flame Candle

Candle making is one way to get the color and scents you desire. Though candles traditionally burn with a red-orange flame, you can change the color of the flame by making slight tweaks to the wick itself. Adding extra items to the wick soaking process is simple and will produce a brilliant green flame which will give your candles a whole new look.

Things you'll need:

- Bucket or container

- Water
- Table salt
- Boric acid
- Copper sulfate
- Clothesline and clothes pins
- Wicks

Directions:

1. Braid together three 12-inch long pieces of cotton yarn or string. Tie a knot at both ends to keep the braid in place. This makes one wick.

2. Dissolve 1/2 tbsp. table salt, 1 tbsp. boric acid and 1 cup of warm water in a glass or disposable plastic bowl. Stir to dissolve the salt and boric acid. Salt and boric acid are used to prime a wick to facilitate even burning.

3. Add 1 extra tsp. of boric acid or copper sulfate to the mix. Stir to dissolve the added minerals to the base mixture. This extra amount of boric acid or copper sulfate will help counteract the orange flame produced by the salt which was used in the process. Boric acid and copper sulfate both burn green.

4. Soak wicks in the solution for 12 to 24 hours. Hang to dry completely on a clothesline and proceed with making candles. The added minerals will emit a green flame while burning.

65

DIY Pillar Candle

Most people think wooden wicks are just for container candles, but did you know, you can use wooden wicks for pillar candles, votives, and tea lights?

When making a pillar candle with a wooden wick, there are a few things you will need to do differently than when using a cotton wick, but if anything, it's easier!

What you'll need:

- Pillar blend wax
- Mold
- Mold sealer

- Fragrance
- Dye (optional)
- Wick, wick clip, glue dot
- Pouring pot
- Thermometer
- Heat gun (optional)
- A good attitude

Directions:

1. Cover the area you will be working on just in case there are any spills or mishaps.
2. Seal the bottom of your mold with mold putty or sealer.
3. Set the wick in the wick clip, attach the wick sticker and place in the bottom center of the mold.
4. Melt your wax to the recommended temperature for your wax blend.
5. Add the dye per manufacturer's instructions.
6. When the wax cools to the suggested pouring temperature for your wax type (refer to the manufacturer's instructions), it is time to add the fragrance. Make sure to spend a couple minutes briskly stirring the fragrance into the wax.
7. Slowly pour the wax into the mold, filling close to the top but being sure to leave at least 1" of the wick above the wax – remember, this is the top of the finished candle and you will need enough wick to do top pours, trim and eventually light.
8. Be sure to poke relief holes as the candle cools.
9. As the candle cools it will shrink and form a dip so it is going to require 2-3 top pours to get an even finish.

10. Once the final pour has been made and the candle has cooled completely, if the surface isn't smooth you can use a heat gun to quickly smooth out the top.
11. Release the candle from the mold, trim the wick to 3/16"

66

DIY Holiday Candle Favors

I made these super easy party favors for guests to take home with them. And you can make 'em too. So quick and easy!

What you'll need:

- Air Wick candles
- Scissors
- Decorative paper

- Washi tape
- Ribbon

Directions:

1. Start by peeling off the easy to remove Air Wick labels for each candle. Customize the glass container anyway you'd like (paint pens, collage, etc) or leave it simple, without embellishments.
2. Then cut out a piece of decorative paper into a square that is several times larger than the candle itself.
3. Next, fold the ends of the paper upward, wrapping the candle completely from the bottom up, but leaving the top open.
4. Wrap a long piece of washi tape around the entire candle to hold the paper in place.
5. Add a ribbon and any other embellishments and you're done.

67

DIY Glitter Pumpkin Candle

In this DIY, I'm using mini-pumpkins leftover from my Halloween decorations and transitioning them into candles that can be used for your Thanksgiving festivities.

What you'll need:

- Mini-pumpkins
- Assorted glitter (make sure it says non-flammable)
- Votive candles
- Plain ole school glue or mod podge (i used elmer's – also non-flammable)
- Knife/ pumpkin saw from carving kits

Directions:

1. Draw circle on top of pumpkin the same size as votive. Carve out the circle just as you would a normal pumpkin.
2. Scoop out the seeds. I used just a kitchen spoon, because you need something small enough to get in the nooks and crannies of the little pumpkin.
3. Apply glue directly to the pumpkin. Sprinkle on desired glitter. *I did this in a number of rounds, letting patches dry, then seeing where I needed to fill in.
4. Let dry overnight.
5. Place votive candle in the center. Enjoy!

68

DIY Fruit Scraps Candle

When it comes to expensive organic produce, I don't like to waste a single scrap. If you have a compost pile, you can always put your fruit and veggie scraps there. Otherwise, I've come up with a few solutions to maximize every inch of your plants.

With my veggie scraps—which include items like carrot tops and kale ribs—I like to make my own veggie stock. You can read more about how I collect and transform the scraps under Basic Formulas.

What you'll need:

- Fruit scraps of any variety (accumulate in the fridge over the course of a day or two) I'm using citrus, kiwi, mango, and apple
- Oil (I'm using vegetable)
- Mason jars of any size
- Oil wicks (You can make your own or purchase in store or online. I'm using wicks with a glass covering)

Directions:

1. Puncture a hole in the lid of your mason jar. The size will depend on the type of wick that you are using. The lid of a mason jar is easy to puncture with just a screwdriver or other metal tool with a semi-sharp tip.
2. Fill the mason jar with your fruit scraps. Cram them in tightly, leaving a small gap in the middle to accommodate your wick. You can arrange them with your fingers or a variety of different kitchen tools. I squished the scraps down with an ice cream scoop myself.
3. Fill the remaining space in the mason jar with oil. Keep in mind that you will need to add the wick, so don't fill it quite to the brim.
4. Thread your wick through the hole you created in the lid and gently push the end of it into the candle itself. I used a skewer to do this.
5. Screw on the lid and wait an hour or two for the wick to absorb the oil before lighting. Don't expect the candles to be immediately scented, although it could happen.

69

DIY Manly Candle

Can't get into the floral smells and garish artwork of storebought candles? Nope, us either. So we came up with our very own DIY version to make a reusable rustic candle that any guy can be proud to burn in his home. (Or log cabin?)

What you'll need:

- Rustic mug or container (try an enamel mug designed for camping, or an old cup from the secondhand store)
- A penny

- Essential oil of your choice
- 1/2 a pound-ish of wax - For this project we used 24 candles from the dollar store. *See more details below.
- Candle wick (you can buy one at your local craft store or you can use one from the melted candles).
- A chopstick or wooden skewer
- A bowl and a saucepan to make a double boiler.

Directions:

1. Make a double boiler by placing a bowl over a pot with water (make sure the water's not touching the bowl). Bring water to a boil and reduce heat so it simmers.
2. Add wax/candles and let them melt. Add a few drops of the essential oil. Stir with a chopstick.
3. While everything is melting - "glue" the penny to the candle wick by using a few drops of wax. Place the penny right in the center of the cup and tie a knot around the chopstick to keep it from moving.
4. *Carefully* start pouring the hot, scented wax into the cup. Save a a bit of wax for any touch ups.
5. The wax will contract a bit while it cools down. If it shrinks too much around the edges, use the left over wax to fill up any holes.
6. Cut the excess wick and light it up!

70

Wine Bottle Drip Candle Holder

Here's a candle craft that I remember from the 1970's, when wine bottles were the candle holders of choice at many parties and coffee houses. Perhaps this mod trend came from candlelit French cafes, where each table was topped by a checkered tablecloth and lit by a tapered candle dripping colored wax over green bottle glass.

What you'll need:

- Glass wine bottles or beer bottles (I used both)
- White spirit

- Gold spray paint
- Masking tape
- Tapered candles

Directions:

1. Clean up your bottles to make sure there's no liquid inside and remove any stubborn sticky labels with white spirit
2. Spray paint them! Try an allover coat or fix masking tape around the middle (which you remove when the paint is dry) for a gold dipped effect. I did 3 light coats on each bottle to stop the paint from streaking.
3. If you're new to spray painting, make sure you cover all the nearby surfaces or paint outside. This stuff gets everywhere! It's also a good idea to keep a window open because the fumes are pretty strong.
4. For small bottle openings, use a knife to chisel the bottom of the candle away into a point. This way you can wedge the candle into the bottle. If the bottle opening is too wide, drip candle wax around the edge to make it narrower.

71

DIY Citronella Beeswax Candle

Citronella oil is commonly used in warding off mosquito. It's a fabulous bug repellent as well as a soother for bug bites! It is a potent anti-fungal as well as antibacterial and antiseptic.

What you'll need:

- Glass containers or jars for your candles
- Beeswax

- Citronella Essential Oil
- Lead Free Wicks
- 2 straws or chopsticks
- A medium sized pot
- A glass pyrex bowl with spout
- A cookie sheet

Directions:

1. Prepare your empty containers by placing a wick in the center of the container and steadying it with 2 straws taped together so that the wick will stay centered. Place in the oven. (170F)
2. Create a double boiler by filling a medium sized pot 1/2 way full with water, place a glass pyrex bowl in the water.
3. Pour beeswax in a glass bowl and allow to fully melt. **keep heat to low-medium**
4. Remove glass bowl from heat and add Citronella. How much depends on how much beeswax you decide to melt. I melted 1 lb. and got 5 candles of different sizes. I added around 80 drops to 1 lb. of beeswax.
5. Pour your beeswax/citronella into glass containers.
6. Steady your wick and allow to cool, preferably in a warm (170F) oven.
7. Trim your wick. (1/4 inch)
8. Allow to set for 48 hours in order to cure before lighting.

72

DIY Wine Bottle Candle

Instead of throwing out those old wine bottles, why turn them into neat, nifty projects? The glass containers are actually a whole lot more versatile than you might think. When it comes to home decor or self-made gifts, there's nothing better than personalized DIY candles that can deliver an all-new look to your room as well as keep your loved ones reminded of you.

What you'll need:

- Old wine bottles
- A bottle glass cutter

- Abrasive paper
- Wicks out of wood* with their holders
- Soya wax granulate*
- Aromatic oil
- A fire proof pot

Directions:

1. Cut your wine bottles with your bottle cutter
2. Melt the wax in a pot until it's runny. Add a few drops of the aromatic oil. Place the wooden wicks at the bottoms of the bottom of the glass containers. The holders keep them in place.
3. Pour the liquid wax into the glass container and make sure the wicks don't move or press them down.
4. Let it harden completely and voilá! Your first Christmas presents are done!

73

DIY Sand Candle

Don't lie, now — we know you've done this before. Remember camp? For those of you unfamiliar with this '70s staple, let's travel back 30 years and get down with this groovy design adventure.

What you'll need:

- Three bowls of different sizes
- A slab of wax
- Wicks

- Metal washers
- A sandbox
- Colored sand
- A ruler

Directions:

1. First, find a sandbox. If you don't have one, dig a hole about 5 inches deep and 12 inches wide. Line it with plastic and fill it with sand.
2. Next, use a double boiler to heat the wax. (The water boils in the bottom pot, melting the wax in the top pot.) Read the directions on the wax package to find the wax's melting temperature. Avoid overheating the wax because it will take longer to solidify.
3. When the wax is melted, wear hot mits and carry it carefully to the sandbox.
4. Make a mold in the sand with a bowl. Press the bowl into the sand about 5 to 6 inches deep.
5. Pour colored sand designs into the mold and make indentions for the wax to fill. Be creative. Pour the hot wax into the finished mold.
6. Place the wick by tying one end around a ruler and the other to a washer. The washer will allow the wick to float to the bottom of the hot wax. The ruler will support the wick over the mold by resting on the rim of the sand.
7. Wait a good three hours before taking the candle out of the mold. Feel the candle to test for firmness. If it is a little bit soft on top, it may not be solid all the way through.

74

DIY Dip Dyed Candle

Candles are a great winter warmer, this year why not try personalizing your candles by giving them the on trend dip dye effect.

Great activity to do with the kids and also makes for a chic centerpiece or decoration. These beautiful candles are also a perfect homemade gift idea. Just choose the favorite colors of a loved one for a thoughtful gift this Christmas!

What you'll need:

- White candles (preferably pillar shape)

- Bleached beeswax beads
- Knife
- Crayons
- Ceramic plate

Directions:

1. Boil some water in a large saucepan and place a bowl or another saucepan into the water to act as a double boiler.
2. Place the bleached beeswax into the saucepan to melt.
3. Add shaving of the crayon of you desired colour. Add more shavings for a bolder colour. Remove wax from heat.
4. You can use an old candle to test the colour. Dip the candle into the hot wax for about 10 seconds then place on a heat proof surface or ceramic plate to cool.
5. Once the wax has completely cooled and solidified you will be able to pop the candle out of the wax and have your finished product.

75

DIY Olive Oil Candle

Olive oil candles burn very small quantities of oil. They are the essence of economical lighting and more affordable than most candles. I love to add a few drops of essential oils like tea tree or lavender to the oil; it smells divine.

What you'll need:

- Cotton oil candle wicks (or some 100% cotton something)
- A vessel for oil (like a half pint glass jar)
- Wire

- Pliers
- Olive oil

Directions:

1. Create the wick holder. To assemble your own olive oil lamp create an apparatus out of the wire for holding the wick. I made a freestanding spiral that holds the wick lightly-pinched though the hole at the top. Careful not to squeeze the wick too tightly because it must stay saturated with oil for efficient burning.

2. You can design a metal hook that hangs from the side of your jar into the olive oil. The side hook method makes the wick easy to lift out and light. Or if you're talented with wire art here's a lasting design perfect for a small jar

3. Adjust wick to burner. Adjust the wick so about 1/4" sticks above the wire burner.

4. Add olive oil. Place your wire wick assembly into your container. Add olive oil just above the top of the wire.

5. Squeeze the tip of the wick slightly to remove extra oil and light it with a match or lighter. It is often easiest to light when the coil is lifted and tilted slightly. The key to burning olive oil is to keep the wick saturated with oil at all times.

76

DIY Ice Candle

Homemade ice candles are such an easy way to decorate outside in the winter weather! I remember making these with my grandparents as a kid (I actually had to call them to get instructions to make them myself this year!).

What you'll need:

- Ice cream pail or other plastic container
- Water

- Butter knife
- Tea light candles (I prefer LEDs)

Directions:

1. Fill a pail with water and set outside to freeze.
2. Allow the water to freeze, but not completely solid. Ensure that ice is at least 1" thick around the edges.
3. You will see bubbles forming inside the frozen mass.
4. Smash centre of cavity with a butter knife and dump the water out. This will be your cavity.
5. Carefully turn the pail over and rub the edges, easing the ice out (if it is really frozen, allow the pail to sit in the kitchen sink for a bit to melt a bit to more easily slide out).
6. Place a candle inside the cavity. You're done!

Conclusion

Candle making is really easy to learn and do if you take your time and learn from your mistakes. Impatient and multi tasking people will probably not make good candle makers unless they lose these attributes. Candle making is not really expensive (so buy the best things you can), is enjoyable and allows you to express your creativity and imagination. In the end, it is also quite enjoyable to sit back and relax and enjoy the fruit of your labors.

Made in United States
Troutdale, OR
11/04/2023